W9-BNW-325

Modern Critical Interpretations

Modern Critical Interpretations

Cervantes's
Don Quixote

Edited and with an introduction by
Harold Bloom
Sterling Professor of the Humanities
Yale University

CHELSEA HOUSE PUBLISHERS
Philadelphia

T23096

© 2001 by Chelsea House Publishers, a subsidiary of
Haights Cross Communications.

Introduction © 2001 by Harold Bloom.

Printed and bound in the United States of America

10 9 8 7 6 5 4 3 2 1

∞ The paper used in this publication meets the minimum
requirements of the American National Standard for
Permanence of Paper for Printed Library Materials,
Z39.48-1984

Library of Congress Cataloging-in-Publication Data

Don Quixote: modern critical interpretations / editor,
Harold Bloom.
     p.   cm. Includes bibliographical references.
     ISBN 0-7910-5922-7 (alk. paper)
     1. Cervantes Saavedra, Miguel de, 1547–1616.
Don Quixote. I. Bloom, Harold.

PQ6352. D67 2000
863'.3—dc21   00-060349
                                     CIP

Chelsea House Publishers
1974 Sproul Road, Suite 400
Broomall, PA 19008-0914

The Chelsea House World Wide Web address is
http://www.chelseahouse.com

Contributing Editor: Mirjana Kalezic

Produced by: Robert Gerson Publisher's Services, Santa Barbara, CA

11/7/02   *$37.95*

Contents

Editor's Note

My Introduction centers upon the authenticity of dialogue between Sancho and the Don, who change one another through mutual listening.

Miguel de Unamuno begins the chronological sequence of essays with his profound meditation upon Don Quixote's will to survive, after which the great novelist Thomas Mann voyages with Cervantes, in order to reveal some of the complex ironies of *Don Quixote*.

Franz Kafka's parable teaches us that Sancho Panza is the poet, and the Don only Sancho's daemon or creation, while Erich Auerbach argues for the book's "continuous gaiety."

The poet W. H. Auden sees Quixote as a fool-for-Christ, after which the novelist Vladimir Nabokov affirms the aestheticism of the book's frequent cruelties.

Jorge Luis Borges, in a brilliant parody, gives us the imaginary Pierre Menard as the author of *Don Quixote*, which is to say that belatedly we all share in the work's authorship.

In Mark Van Doren's view, the Don's quest is as realistic as it is comic, while Harry Levin emphasizes the ambiguous relations between words and deeds in the book.

José Ortega y Gasset regards Don Quixote as a hero for whom reality is a challenge to reform, while my own, concluding essay insists that the Don's is a *literary* madness, and so in itself represents a triumph of Cervantes's comic wisdom.

Introduction

*D*on *Quixote* is to the Spanish language what Shakespeare is to English, Dante to Italian, and Goethe to German: the glory of that particular vernacular. There is no similar singular eminence in French: Rabelais, Montaigne, Molière, and Racine vie with Victor Hugo, Baudelaire, Stendhal, Balzac, Flaubert, and Proust. Perhaps Cervantes's masterwork is the central book of the last half-millennium, since all the greater novelists are as much *Don Quixote*'s children as they are Shakespeare's. As I have remarked elsewhere, Shakespeare pragmatically teaches us how to talk to ourselves, while Cervantes instructs us how to talk to one another. Hamlet scarcely listens to what anyone else says (except it be the Ghost), while Falstaff so delights himself that Prince Hal can seem merely the best of resentful students and half-voluntary audiences. But Don Quixote and Sancho Panza change and mature by listening to one another, and their friendship is the most persuasive in all of literature.

Don Quixote or Hamlet? Sancho Panza or Falstaff? The choice would be difficult. But Hamlet has only Horatio, and Falstaff ends in solitude, dying while playing with flowers and evidently dreaming of the table promised in Psalm 23, to be prepared for one by God in the midst of one's enemies. Don Quixote dies in Sancho's loving company, with the wise squire proposing fresh quests to the heroic knight. Perhaps Shakespeare did invent the ever-growing inner self, compelled to be its own adventure, as Emily Dickinson (an authentic heir of Shakespeare) proclaimed. Cervantes, whose life was arduous and darkly solitary, was able to achieve a miracle that Shakespeare evaded. Where in Shakespeare can we find two great natures in full communion with each other? Antony and Cleopatra are giant forms, but they never listen to what anyone else says, including one another. Lady Macbeth fades out, Lear is most himself addressing the heavens, while Prospero has no human peer. I fantasize sometimes that Shakespeare, in eternity, brings together his most vital characters upon one

1

stage: Falstaff, Hamlet, Rosalind, Iago, Lear, Macbeth, Cleopatra. But in this life, he chose otherwise.

The reader needs no better company than Sancho and the Don: to make a third with them is to be blessed with happiness, yet also to be favored with self-insight. The Don and Sancho, between them, know all that there is to know. They know at last exactly who they are, which is what, finally, they will teach the rest of us.

MIGUEL DE UNAMUNO

Glosses on Don Quixote

I. The Essence of Quixotism

Every madman is driven mad by his sanity; I mean to say that the madman raves and rants about the same things which would preoccupy him were he sane; and, strictly speaking, on this head the sane and insane are scarcely to be distinguished, since the former think the same mad thoughts as the latter, and only avoid declaring them or acting them out.

With this in mind, let us attempt to discover the essence of Don Quixote's madness; for this purpose I should like to avail myself of four passages from the eternal narrative of his adventures, just as I might avail myself of forty others.

> Now that his reason had completely flown, he lit upon the oddest notion ever to strike a madman in this world, so that it seemed to him only right and even necessary, as much for the *increase of his honor* as for the service of his country, that he should turn knight-errant and go about the world, armed and on horseback, in search of adventures and exercising himself in all those endeavors he had read about in books of chivalry as the common exercise of knights, undoing all manner of wrong and placing himself in situations and perils from whose overcoming *he would gain eternal name and fame* (Part One, Chapter 1).

From *Our Lord Don Quixote: The Life of Don Quixote and Sancho with Related Essays.* © 1967 by the Bollingen Foundation.

Here we see clearly that the essence of his madness is that which elsewhere, in my novel *Amor y pedagogía*, I called "herostratism," the mad craving for immortality which, should we doubt of living on in spirit, makes us long to leave behind at lest our *eternal name and fame*.

Poor Alonso Quixano was driven mad by reading books of chivalry, and he fell into the folly of wanting to appear in their pages, of wanting to have the history of his adventures written down there so that he should gain eternal name and fame. Thus we find him, as he takes to the open field in his first sally, talking to himself as he rides along and saying: "Who can doubt but that in ages to come, when the true history of my famous deeds comes to light . . . ?" and all the rest of it. The same obsession follows him through the course of all his adventures.

When he was bested by the Knight of the White Moon and was returning home to his village to carry out the penance his enemy had imposed upon him, he arrived at the meadow on the road to Zaragoza where formerly he had encountered "gay shepherdesses and gallant shepherds who there proposed to revive and imitate the pastoral Arcadia, an intention as novel as it was ingenious," and there he proposed to Sancho that they become shepherds, buy some sheep and "everything else needful for the pastoral office"; that he, Don Quixote, call himself the shepherd Quixotiz, while Sancho Panza be known as the shepherd Pancino, and they go about the woods and dales singing and idling. And he finished his suggestion saying that by such a way of life they would become "famous and eternal, not only in the present, but for centuries to come" (Part Two, Chapter 67).

It has been truly said that each madman has his theme. Alonso Quixano here seems to change his madness, but its essence remains with him, for if he became a knight-errant in order to win eternal name and fame, he now thinks to turn Arcadian shepherd so as to become eternal and famous, not only in present times, but in ages to come.

And poor Quixano the Good did not ever lose sight of the malign root of his madness, as we see in one of the most beautiful passages—to my taste, the most beautiful—of his wandering history. When he finds himself at last in the open country, free and disburdened of the demands and attentions of Altisidora (Part Two, Chapter 58), he encounters some peasants carrying wooden images for the altar of their village church; the carved statues represent Saint George, Saint Martin, Saint James the Moor-Slayer, and Saint Paul, and after pondering the merits of these four knights-errant Don Quixote proclaims: "These saints and knights professed, even as I do, the calling of arms. The difference between us is that they were saints and fought divinely, while I am a sinner and fight humanly." And he adds these most pregnant words: "They conquered heaven by force of arms because heaven suffers violence, but as for me, I don't know to this moment what it is that I conquer by force of my feats and travail. If my Dulcinea del Toboso could be freed from her own travails, and my fortune were to improve and my wits be mended, it might be that I could tread a better path than the one I'm on."

At this brief moment of descent to prudence and his own sanity, Don Quixote lets us see that he was conscious of the root of his madness. I am personally not one of those who suppose that the work of Cervantes possesses any esoteric sense whatever, or that he sought to embody symbols in the characters of his story, but I do believe that we have a right to see our own symbols in these characters.

For me, Dulcinea del Toboso has always symbolized glory, that is, worldly glory, the inextinguishable thirst to leave behind eternal name and fame in the world. The ingenious hidalgo declares, in his fit of sanity, that if he were perhaps to be cured of his thirst for glory, for worldly renown and fame, he would direct his steps toward attaining that other glory, in which his faith as an Old Christian made him believe.

And I come to the fourth passage, on the sublime death of the sublime madman, to the time when, freed from the misty shadows of the ignorance in which he labored as a consequence of his grievous and continual reading of those detestable books of chivalry, he confesses his fault, confesses his folly, and admits the risk he had run by reading such books; and, putting aside the fairy stories which had been true only in truly damaging his mind, he makes his own death turn them, with the help of heaven, to his advantage. Alonso Quixano dies "repentant" of his madness, repenting it not as a deplorable misfortune but as a sin, and he dies convinced of his culpability. And a sin his madness was, according to his Christian point of view, because it stemmed from vainglory, from the tormenting thirst for eternal renown, from herostratism.

The passion to survive stifled in Don Quixote the enjoyment of life, a capacity for enjoyment that is characteristic of Sancho. Sancho's wisdom was the result of his holding on to this life and this world in the measure that he could personally enjoy them, and the sanchopanzesque heroism—for Panza is heroic—consisted in his following a madman, being himself sound of mind, an action more filled with faith than that of a madman following his own madness.

Great was Don Quixote's madness, and it was great because the root from which it grew was great: the inextinguishable longing to survive, a source of the most extravagant follies as well as of the most heroic acts. The outstanding benefactors of their fatherland and of their fellow men have been those who dreamed of eternal name and fame.

But, the truth is, there are two classes of ambitious men: those who have faith in themselves and those who have none at all. In those who are not equipped with a firm faith in themselves, the thirst for notoriety, or at least for renown, engenders envy and produces the sad figure of the frustrated man. Nothing more lamentable than a Quixote who, not believing that the windmills are giants, cannot make up his mind to take to the field, lance under arm and helmet on his head.

History knows of a memorable type of herostratism: that disciple of Cola Montano, Girolamo Olgiati by name, who along with two others assassinated Galeazzo Sforza, the tyrant of Milan. Olgiati, Lampugnani, and Visconti met together in the church of San Stefano under cover of night, formed a conspiracy, and, after seeking aid from St. Ambrose, patron saint of Milan, whose image stood before them, vowed to kill the tyrant, and killed him. As he was being led to his own death on the scaffold shortly after, Girolamo Olgiati exclaimed: "Courage, Girolamo, you will be remembered for ages to come! Death is bitter, but fame is eternal!"

But nowhere have I read a more quintessential, concentrated, lively, or powerful expression of the root-quality of quixotism, of the absurd anxiety for eternal renown, than in a passage from one of our own dramatists, in a drama that is itself a marvel of concentrated vivacity and expressive force, *Las mocedades del Cid*, by Guillén de Castro, in which, as Rodrigo Arias falls dead in a duel, he pronounces these final words: "Death to me! Long live my fame!"

To sacrifice oneself to one's fame rather than to sacrifice one's fame to oneself: herein lies the quintessence of quixotism and the root of its heroism. Life may be a dream, but I, the dreamer who dreams it, I am no dream, even though Shakespeare tells us that we are such stuff as dreams are made on. Nor is it true that he whose fame lives on really and truly dies.

It would be worth the effort it would take to trace through Spanish history the workings of quixotism, and to see on the other hand how we have been brought to the sorry pass we are in by the fact that those who are taken for ambitious among us place all their hopes and ambition on achieving prestige and power while they still live, and exclusively within the confines of our own country, at that. This attitude, and no other, is the essence of sanchopanzism; an ambition which is allayed by the governorship of an Isle of Barataria. Men of such moderate ambitions may perhaps be more prudent than men of unbridled ambitions, than truly quixotic men, but the fatherland ought not pay them a rental fee for their shrewdness.

To Alonso Quixano it seemed reasonable and even necessary for the greater glory of his honor, that is, of his fame, as well as for the service of his country, that he should become a knight-errant. The best servants of their country are those who take pains to increase its honor, and the wider the space and the longer the time they covet for their fame and renown, so much the greater will be the force with which they serve their country.

"Death to me! Long live my fame!"

II. The Cause of Quixotism

In speaking of the essence of Quixotism I said that it consisted of a longing for eternal name and fame, of a longing for immortality. To which I should add that Cervantes himself felt this longing in the depths of his own being. As he brought his everlasting work to a conclusion he wrote, addressing himself to his pen: "Here you shall rest, hanging from the rack by this bit of copper wire, whether well- or ill-cut, my goose-quill, I do not know. And there you shall stay for long centuries. . . ." And then: "For me alone was Don Quixote born, and I for him; he knew how to act, and I to write." Cervantes himself longed for the perpetuation of his name and fame.

And it is natural that Cervantes should find Don Quixote in the secret recesses of his own soul, that he should dredge him out of the depths of his own spirit. It has been repeated often with great justice that Don Quixote is Cervantes himself. He is Cervantes in the measure that the latter was a man of his time and people, he is the Spanish soul incarnated in Cervantes. And in this soul he represents the longing to leave behind a name.

This longing to leave behind eternal name and fame is no more than one form of the thirst for immortality that animates all those who are in love with life.

I believe it to be an error, in speaking of the so-called Spanish cult of death, to assert that we do not love life because we find it hard on us, or to say that the Spaniard has never felt a great attachment to life. On the contrary, I believe he has felt a great attachment to life, precisely because it is hard on him, and that from his intense attachment to life springs what we call his cult of death.

Our love of life is so great that we want it to last forever, without end, and we cannot resign ourselves to losing it, so that the hope of living on, or the fear of not surviving stifles in us the enjoyment of life, that *joie de vivre* which so thoroughly characterizes the French.

If some people will protest that they cannot comfort themselves with hope nor torment themselves with fear because they lack faith in their own survival and because they are completely convinced that, on the death of each one of us, all our consciousness comes to an end, I reply that their desire to survive is not killed by their conviction of the impossibility of its coming to pass, but that on the contrary, it is their very small urge to go on living that deprives them of faith in living on.

In the Third Part of the *Ethics* of Spinoza, who was a Jew of Spanish origin—or Portuguese; for our purposes it makes no difference—there are four admirable propositions, the sixth, seventh, eighth, and ninth, where he establishes that the real essence of everything consists of its tendency or endeavor to persist in its own proper being for an indefinite time, and that the human mind is conscious of this tendency on its own part. Schopenhauer's doctrine of the will is a development of this marvelous passage. And if Schopenhauer felt the admiration he did for the Spanish and held us to be a people of robust will—in contradiction to the contrary view, so prevalent among ourselves—it was because he saw our tremendous zeal to persist individually, without end or termination, and appreciated our thirst for immortality.

This thirst stems, I repeat, from an intense attachment to life, concrete and lived and loved, and not merely the spectacle of the passing show.

Strictly speaking, then, it is the poverty of life that, engendering a profound attachment to it, at the same time gives rise to the longing for immortality; the poverty of life, accompanied by leisure; for a poor and arduous life, hardship in the midst of poverty, produces only sanchopanzism.

Sancho Panza was a poor peasant, a poor laborer, absorbed in the chores of the fields, and Don Quixote was a poor and idle hidalgo.

There are few more admirable pages than those that open *Don Quixote*, where Cervantes, in order to explain the madness of his hero and tell us how his brain withered up from his reading, begins by detailing how the nobleman ate and lived.

"A pot of somewhat more beef than lamb, hash on most nights, near fast and scraps on Saturdays, lentils on Fridays, a pigeon as a bit of a treat on Sundays, consumed more than three-fourths of his income. The rest maintained a wardrobe consisting of a broadcloth doublet, velvet breeches for holidays, a pair of slippers to match, and a fine homespun suit of the best for the middle of the week."

The fasts and scraps on Saturdays explain the hidalgo's attachment to life. He was also "an early riser by nature and fond of the hunt," although "whenever he was idle—which was on most days of the year—he gave himself up to reading books of chivalry, which he did with such fondness and gusto that he almost entirely forgot his hunting and even the care of his estate; his fond foolishness reached such a peak that he sold many acres of crop land so as to buy more books of chivalry. . . ."

To the fasts and scraps of Saturday, to the poverty of the ingenious hidalgo, must be added his idleness, for he was idle on most days of the year. And his poverty was such that he was forced to sell many acres of crop land in order to be able to read the books with which he filled his leisure time. An idle and poor gentleman, he grew very attached to life, and since life was hard and monotonous in his poor Manchegan hamlet, he thirsted for a more ample life, a life everlasting in the eternity of his name and fame.

A thesis a thousand times sustained, and almost always with justification, is that the harshness and asperity of life only serves to increase our love for it, while the terrible affliction of *taedium vitae* is born of satiety. I am just now reading the admirable essays that make up the book titled *The Will to Believe and Other Essays in Popular Philosophy* by the vigorous American philosopher William James, and there is one among them called "Is Life Worth Living?" in which the author skillfully develops the point that the source of melancholy lies in satiation, that necessities and struggle inspire us, and that it is in the hour of triumph that we must face emptiness. "Not the Jews of the captivity," he says, "but those of the days of Solomon's glory are those from whom the pessimistic utterances in our Bible come."

The terrible cry "Vanity of vanities, all is vanity!" is in effect a complaint breathed forth from satiety. Whoever, like Sancho Panza, lives bent over the earth, struggling to wrest from it, day by day and grain by grain, the bread which sustains him, does not vilify life but rather yearns for peace and rest in it—and not outside it—and dreams of good fortune and glut on the Isle of Barataria. He is lured along by the promise of splendid rewards and the prospect of a life of ease and idleness. He accepts all chores on condition that he be finally rid of work. Thus it was, by the promise that "perhaps some adventure or other might befall him, and that he might, in the twinkling of an eye, win some island and be made governor of it," that Don Quixote dragged after him his peasant neighbor, that "honest man—if a poor man can ever be called by such a title" (Part One, Chapter 7).

There are few lovers of life so urgent and constant in their love as Sancho Panza. And there is scarcely a sign—at least, I can recall none—to indicate that he rendered any cult to death.

And if Sancho offers us the type of poor and busy workman, Don Quixote is the type of poor and unoccupied idler. His idleness and his poverty explain his attachment to life and his longing to live on and perpetuate himself in books. The busy rich man is never a Sancho Panza, and the idle rich man is never a Don Quixote. The busy rich man is likely to be a philistine, and the idle rich man may be an aesthete, or a melancholic, or he may be any of a dozen forms of skeptic, possessed by an inner despair borne with greater or lesser resignation.

With great perspicacity, another American, Frank Wadleigh Chandler (in a doctoral thesis on the theme of our picaresque novel, entitled *Romances of Roguery* and presented at Columbia University in 1899) notes how at the beginning of our decadence, "as the courage of the paladin was replaced by the clever cowardice of the pickpocket, so the war against monsters and enchantments succumbed to the common conflict against hunger and thirst." But, was not the war against monsters and enchantments one form of the conflict against hunger and thirst? And how did Don Quixote degenerate into the rogue Guzmán de Alfarache?

Don Quixote's poverty was merely relative, for the fasts and scraps of Saturdays were compensated, in part, by the hash on most nights, the lentils on Fridays, and the pigeon as a bit of a treat on Sundays, and he still had acres of crop land left, though his estate was small, to use for the purchase of books of chivalry. If his poverty had been greater, such that it would not have allowed him the opportunity to fill his head with the absurdities and follies of his books, nor even have permitted him to go off hunting at the break of dawn, then he would have had to set out alone, without appurtenances and without a horse, without a squire, or lance, or helmet, and find a life for himself in the towns and hamlets as best God gave him means. Impoverish poor Alonso Quixano a bit more and you make him into Guzmán de Alfarache; which is not to depreciate the former, but rather to exalt the latter, for our rogues were possessed of a basic and generous quixotism, even if their need to earn a living did not allow them to think much about gaining eternal name and fame, a type of thinking which demands some leisure for it to flower.

The end of the ascent is the beginning of the descent, as the notably precise platitude puts it. And so in the very womb of the period which is known as the time of our Spanish grandeur, the signs of decadence are already to be noted. In the same manner, in the womb of Quixotism, we can detect the elements of the picaresque; and it is not necessary to be a lynx, nor anything like one, to observe in the course of the ingenious Knight's adventures that he possessed a picaresque side to his character: notably, his tendency to live at the cost of his neighbors, even though his parasitism was founded on the belief that everything was his due because of the useful and patriotic nature of the career of knight-errantry which he had elected.

The roguish side of Don Quixote, his picaresquesness, deserves a special essay, and special consideration on the basis of selected passages from our national Bible.

It is a great shame that though an infinitude of scholars and Masoretes have fallen upon *Don Quixote*, and have scrutinized every nook and cranny of the text, submitting it to every form of historical examination and exegesis— and some of the exegetes have been not a whit less mad than Don Quixote was himself—and though they have found every manner of enigma, arcanum, and intricate symbolism, so few of them have assimilated the spirit of the book or taken advantage of the marvelous history as a text for sermons or a basis for patriotic meditations in the manner that versicles from the Gospel are used for making homilies, sermons, and pious counsels for a better and more inward life. As much as we may meditate on *Don Quixote*, as the Greeks meditated on the Homeric poems or the English on the dramas of Shakespeare, we cannot consume all the marrow of wisdom that it contains.

THOMAS MANN

Voyage with Don Quixote

May nineteenth, 1934. It seemed a good idea to begin it by drinking a vermouth in the bar; accordingly we did so, while quietly awaiting the moment when the ship should start. I had taken out of my travelling-bag this notebook and one of the four little orange linen volumes of *Don Quixote*, the chosen companions of my trip. More unpacking was uncalled for at the moment. We had nine or ten days before us until we should land on the other side of the world. Another Saturday would come round, another Monday and Tuesday, before this well-conducted adventure of ours should reach its goal. The easy-going Dutch boat whose gangplank we had just mounted does not do it faster—why should she? The speed corresponding to her comfortable medium size is certainly saner and more natural than the shattering, record-breaking pace of those colossi which in six or even four days madly overlap the vast spaces that lie before us. *Piano, piano!* Richard Wagner thought that *andante* was the true German tempo. Well, there is something very arbitrary about all these half-way answers to the question "What is German?" And in the end it remains unsettled, leaving a negative impression because they appear to condemn as un-German all sorts of things that are not so at all—as, for instance, the *allegretto*, the *scherzo, and the sprituoso!* This remark of Wagner's would have been happier if he had left out all reference to the national—a sentimentalizing idea anyhow—and confined himself to the objective value that I ascribe to the quality of slowness. All good things take time; so do all great things. In other words, space will have its time. It is a familiar feeling with me that there is a sort of *hubris*, and a great superficiality, in those who would take away from space or stint it of the time naturally bound up with it. Goethe, who was certainly a friend of man, yet did not like to use artificial aids to his powers of perception, such as the microscope and telescope, would probably have agreed with this scruple. Of course, the question arises where the line is to be drawn and whether ten days are not just as bad as six or four. To be strictly orthodox, one would have to give the ocean as many weeks instead, and travel by the wind, which is a force of nature, just as steam is. As a matter of fact, we are using oil fuel. But these speculations approach the fantastic.

And yet my flights of fancy are explainable enough: their source is my own inward excitement. I have, quite simply, stage fright. And what wonder? My maiden voyage across the Atlantic, my first encounter with the mighty ocean, my first knowledge of it—and there, on the other side of the curvature of the earth, above which the great waters heave, New Amsterdam the metropolis awaits us! There are only four or five such in the world, only four or five of this unique and monstrous breed of cities, extravagant in size and kind, standing out even among what we call capital cities, just as in the natural kingdom, among the features of the landscape, the mountain, the desert, and the ocean belong in a category by themselves. I grew up on the Baltic, a provincial body of water. And the traditions of my blood are those of the small and old-established city, civilized and gentled, whose inhabitants are endowed with sensitive imaginations and capable of feeling for the elemental both a sense of awe and a sort of ironic distaste. Ivan Goncharov was once on the high seas during a violent storm. The captain had him fetched from his cabin to behold it: Goncharov was a writer, he said, the storm was magnificent, he ought not to miss it. The author of *Oblomov* came on deck, looked about him, and said: "Yes, it's a nuisance, isn't it?" And went below again.

It is soothing to realize that we are to confront the welter under the ægis of civilization and with all the protection it can afford. This stout ship, of whose white and shining stateroom doors, promenade decks, lounges, and carpeted flights of stairs we have just had a hasty view, she will carry us through, she and the officers and crew whose one mission in life it is to command the elements. She reminded me of that white train *de luxe* with the blue window-panes in which the traveller to Khartoum is borne through the grey waste, among the glowing hot, death-breathing hills of the Libyan and Arabian deserts. . . . Exposure: one has but to think the word, to realize all it means to live in the shelter of our human civilization. I have small respect for the man who, confronting elemental nature, has nothing to express but a pæan of admiration and feels her insensate hostility not at all.

And then, the season itself sets bounds to that hostility and greatly mitigates the perils of our adventure. Spring is far advanced; we need not anticipate any very extravagant misbehaviour on the part of the ocean. We hope that our sea-legs will stand the strain of the moderate demands that may be put upon them. And besides, have we not certain tablets tucked away in our hand-bags as a last resort for human frailty? In the winter-time it would be far otherwise. Friends of mine, artists on concert tour, have told me of the mingled terrors and absurdities of such a voyage. These we are not likely to be called upon to endure. The waves are mountains. They are Everests. No one may go on deck. The fretful Goncharov would not be dragged from his cabin and, anyhow, one can see the ocean better through the thick glass bull's-eye of the port-hole. You lie barricaded in your bed, you get up and fall down again—it is like nothing so much as the racking torments that pass for amusements at fun-fairs, for instance the switchback railway, destructive alike to nerves and digestion. From a giddy height you see your wash-stand swoop down upon you, while on the sloping, shifting floor your cannoning trunks perform a clumsy dance. There is a frightful, an infernal din, caused partly by the elements raging without and partly by the struggles of the labouring ship, trembling and throbbing all over as she pushes on. This may last three days and three nights. Imagine that you have two such behind you and are enduring the third. So far you have taken no food; the moment comes when you remember that one must eat. Since you have not died, though for hours together you have been quite resigned to go, the time comes when you are hungry. You summon the steward, for the bell still rings and the whole first-class hotel service of the ship still functions amid the general dissolution, disciplined to the very end. Such is the refined and admirable heroism of civilized human beings. The man comes, white-jacketed, table-napkined. He does not fall into the stateroom but stands erect in the doorway. He grasps your faint commands through the roaring of the gale. He goes and comes again, preserving by the swaying, yielding motion of his arms the sore-threatened equilibrium of his covered dishes. He must await a certain moment when the state of things in the universe will abet his depositing your tray, in a curve which he does not control but uses to serve his turn, upon your bed. He sees his moment, seizes it, behaves with resolution and discretion. He seems to be succeeding. But in that moment the outer universe changes its mind and the curve described by your tray deposits its contents upside down on your wife's bed. It is really impossible. . . .

Such are the tales I have heard, they come into my head while we drink our farewell vermouth and I scribble these lines. And why not? Though certainly I do not need them to heighten the respect I feel in the face of our undertaking, for I am respectful by nature; I wear, so to speak, my eyebrows permanently lifted. This is not the attitude of the cosmopolite, but of the provincial with a talent for fantasy inborn. With this gift a man can never be a cosmopolite, since up to old age it saves him, if I may use the flattering word, from any sense of superiority. To have the art of fantasy does not mean that one is able to think something out to a conclusion. It means to *make* something out of things—which, of course, is not cosmopolitan.—We are most suprisingly in act to repeat the voyage of Columbus. For days and nights we shall hover in cosmic space between two continents—even though with first-class service all the time—and I scarcely believe that our fellow passengers are having any thoughts on the subject; certainly not this thought. And anyhow, where are they? We are alone in the bar, whose spaciousness, decked with stamped leather, yawns invitingly at us. And I suddenly recollect that even on the tender which brought us across the bay from Boulogne-sur-Mer, we were as good as alone. The bar steward says that only four passengers including ourselves embarked at Boulogne; some dozen more came on at Rotterdam, while another four would turn up at Southampton. That was all. What did we think of that? We answered that the line must lose a pretty penny on such a voyage. Yes, it was bad; of course, it was "the depression." But on the eastbound trip, we agreed, things would look up. The European season for Americans began in June: Salzburg, Bayreuth, Oberammergau beckoned, there would be plenty—he did not say of what, but implied tips. He looked a good deal disturbed, but professed himself satisfied that the harvest would not be too bad. We for our part ventured the remark that it would be very pleasant to travel on a nearly empty ship. It would belong to us almost altogether; life would be like that on a private yacht. And the thought of all that undisturbed tranquillity brought me back to the reading I meant to do on the voyage, to the little orange-coloured volume lying beside me, the first of the row below-stairs.

Shipboard reading—it falls into a category generally despised. The usual view is that reading for a journey must be of the lightest and shallowest, mere foolery to pass the time. I cannot understand it. In the first place, this so-called light reading is the dullest stuff in the world; but even aside from that I cannot see why, especially upon a serious occasion like this voyage, one should decline below the level of one's intellectual habits and go in for the silly and jejune. Perhaps the conditions of life on shipboard, at once removed from the everyday and full of excitement, produce a mental and nervous condition in which silliness disgusts us less than usual. I was just now talking about respect. Since I have respect for this enterprise of ours, it is right and proper that I also take heed to the reading that accompanies it. *Don Quixote* is universal; just the right reading for a trip to the end of the world. It was no small adventure to write it; the passive adventure of reading it will worthily correspond. Strangely enough, I have never gone through the masterpiece systematically, from beginning to end. I will do so on board and in ten days come to the rim of this ocean of a book, at the same time as we come to the other rim of the Atlantic.

The windlass was making a din as I wrote down this resolve. We went on deck, to look back and forward.

May twentieth. I ought not to do what I am doing: sitting bent over to write. It is not conducive to well-being, for the sea is, as our American table-mates say, "a little rough," and though I agree that our ship moves quietly and steadily, yet her motions are more felt up here on this deck where the writing-room is than they are below. Nor is looking through the window advisable, for the rising and falling of the horizon attacks the head in a way well known from an earlier experience but forgotten until now. Also it is not very healthy to gaze down upon paper and script. Curiously, obstinately persevering is the old habit of settling to composition so soon as breakfast and the morning stroll are over. It persists under the most contrary circumstances.

Last night we stopped awhile outside Southampton and took on a few passengers—our last stop, for now the great unbroken journey lies before us. We have covered considerable distance in the night. The south coast of England is still faintly visible in the dim air; soon it will disappear and we shall have before us only the foam-laced vacant grey margin of the sea, beneath a sky equally vacant and grey. I already knew that the sea, in all its extent, seen from shipboard, makes upon me nothing like the impression I get from the beach. I feel none of the thrill of which I am sensible when I stand on solid ground and hear its long-loved roll. It is a disenchantment, and the reason is not far to seek. We have reduced the element to the status of highroad and railway, deprived it of its character of scenery, dream, idea, imaginary peep into eternity—in short, we have made a setting of it. A setting does not have aesthetic character—that belongs to the picture itself. Schopenhauer says: "Certainly it is beautiful to see things, but not beautiful at all to be things." It is quite possible that the truth of this remark, directed as it is against all longing of every sort, had a connection with my experience of the sea. It is not favourable to any illusion to become intimate with its object. Especially when you do it amid all the disgraceful comfort of first class.

Even so, some demands are still made upon you. There is the unavoidable nervous shock of those first hours after you have lost the solid ground under your feet in exchange for an unstable footing. For days you cannot credit the reality of walking down a staircase that has a wavy motion and lightly rises and falls beneath you. You hold your whirling and protesting head and would like to take the thing as a bad joke.—An absurd walk this morning on deck: a series of paralysed clingings and clutchings, interspersed with drunken plungings which, curiously enough, you accompany by deprecating head-shakes as though you really were in that undignified condition—just as one is prone to feel one's feet heavy when mounting a hill. Yet I rejoiced to be convinced that whatever discomfort it gave me, whatever hyperacidity or nervous upset, yet nothing can affect my love of the salt sea, which has endured since my childhood and is in my blood. Seasickness has nothing to do with it, since it leaves the mind intact and often the appetite as well! So I do not take the sea amiss, and would still be loyal to her, I think, even were my sufferings vastly more acute.

> O thou wild friend of my youth,
> We find each other once more!

—I recalled this morning the lines that Tonio Kröger could not finish, for his throbbing heart.

With symptoms of seasickness must also be reckoned the sleepiness, the utter craving to slumber, which one feels in the first days of a sea voyage. The high atmospheric pressure may be accountable, but surely even more the rocking motion of the boat, which lulls and confuses the brain—an ancient invention of nurses and nursemaids, old as the hills and, like the gifts of the poppy, not of a very innocent kind.

Yesterday afternoon, and last night in the blue salon, to the accompaniment of the music, I read *Don Quixote*. I will now continue to read, sitting in my deck-chair, a transmogrification of Hans Castorp's excellent reclining-chair. What a unique monument is this book! More conditioned in taste by its time than the deliberate satire against that taste would indicate; the whole spirit of the work utterly sycophantic in its protestations of loyalty; yet how its creative genius, critical, free, and human, soars above its age! Tieck's translation, the spirited medium of the classic romantic period, enchants me more than I can say. It is a beautiful instrument wherewith to render the spacious humour of this style—which is almost impressive enough to make me wonder whether humour after all is not the great essential element of the epic. Or even to make me consider them one and the same, though the statement could probably not be objectively sustained. A style that mingles the humorous and the romantic is surely well calculated to make the whole "great and remarkable historie" pass as a translation and commentary of an Arabic manuscript composed by a Moor, Cid Hamete

Benengeli. Upon this manuscript the translator is supposed to base his tale. Indeed, the story often employs the indirect form; as, for instance, he will say: "The story goes on to tell" or "'Allah be praised!' cried out Benengeli three times at the beginning of this chapter, after which he continued," and so forth. Immensely funny are the summary chapter-heads: "Of the wise and pleasant discourse which passed between Sancho Panza and his wife Teresa Panza, as well as other matters worthy of record"; or, with burlesque humour: "Of things which Benengeli says, he will learn who reads them, if he reads with attention." Humorous, finally, in the highest sense, is the portrayal of the two principals, so human and lively is the author's perception of character in all its many-sidedness and depth. He himself is proudly aware of this excellence, when he dwells on the despised and worthless sequel to his first part. This sequel was the work of an impudent bungler, who was tempted by the world-wide fame of Cervantes's novel to seek success with a continuation of it. The plagiary drove Cervantes to compose a second part himself, books seven to twelve in the completed work—though, as Goethe remarks, the theme was really exhausted in the first part. The author of the first sequel saw in Don Quixote naught but a gaby whom only the lash could cure of his delusions, in Sancho Panza merely a glutton. In more than one place in the second part of the true sequel Cervantes protests with jealous scorn against such a simplification. Likewise he embarks upon controversy, which is a model of dignity and moderation, though only in form. It needs the aid of rhetoric to incite a reader to take up the cudgels, while at the same time to preserve a dignity worthy of the man from La Mancha himself. "You would like it well, were I to attack him [the author of the false second part] with adjectives like 'silly,' 'impudent,' 'limited.' But it does not occur to me. His sin be on his own head; he has to answer to himself for what he has done, and that is the end of the matter." Very Christlike and very scrupulous. What really galls Cervantes is simply that "this gentleman" calls him an old cripple—as though it were in the power of genius to hold back time that it should not go over his head; or as though he had got his mutilated hand in a tavern brawl and not in the glorious day of battle (referring to the naval battle of Lepanto). "And besides," he says with spirit, "we assume that a man composes not with his grey hairs but with his understanding, the which commonly improves with the years." That is delightful. But all the mildness and enlightenment of his grey hairs do not prevent him from setting forth the coarsest and most offensive tales to the reader as "the gentleman's" work, and as evidence that it is "one of the most devilish of the Devil's wiles to put it into a man's head that he too can write a book and get it printed and gain money and fame by it." Certainly they betray anger, furious hatred, and a spirit of revenge, these tales; they betray the half-unconscious pain of the artist when he sees confusion in men's minds between that which has success although it is good and that which has success because it is bad.

For it befell Cervantes that a plagiarism that gave itself out as a sequel to his book "went all over the world" and was as eagerly read as the original. It imitated the grosser and more popular qualities of the genuine work, seizing upon the folly of the hero and its inevitable nemesis, as well as upon the gluttony of Sancho Panza. But that was all. It could not attain to the deep human feeling, the melancholy, or the great art—nor, frightful to say, were these much missed. The public, it seems, saw no difference between the two versions. That is depressing for an author. When Cervantes talks about the disgust, the bad taste in his mouth, felt by the reader of the pseudo-*Quixote*, he is speaking for himself and not for his public. He had to write the second part to drive away the bad taste, not from his readers' mouths, but from his own; and it came there not alone from the badness of the performance but also on account of the success of his own first part. The reader must remember that the second part, "written down by the same artist and from the same matter" as the first, was composed in order to rehabilitate the success of the earlier one, to rescue its endangered honour. The second part has no longer the happy freshness and carelessness of the first, which shows how, *par hasard et par génie*, a blithe and vigorous satire grew into the book of a whole people and of all humanity. It would be less weighted down with humanism, cultural elements, and a certain literary frigidity if the ambition to achieve distinction had not played a part in its composition. But in especial the author labours in the second volume to bring out more clearly and consciously that depth and diversity in his delineation of the main characters of which I have already spoken. In this above all he would bear witness to "the same artist and the same matter" as in the first volume. Don Quixote is of course a simpleton; that is clear from his mania of knight-errantry. But his obsolete whimsy is also the source of such true nobility, such purity of life, such an aristocratic bearing, such winning and respect-compelling traits, physical and mental, that our laughter over his grotesque and doleful countenance is always mingled with amazed respect. No one can know him and not feel drawn to the high-minded and pathetic man, mad in one single point but in all others a blameless knight. It is pure spirit, disguised as fantasy, that sustains and ennobles him, that carries his moral dignity unscathed out of each and every humiliation. I find it exquisite that Sancho Panza the pot-bellied, with his proverbs, his mother wit, his shrewd peasant judgment of human nature, who has no use for the "idea" that results in beatings, but rather for the skin of liquor—Sancho Panza has feeling for this spirit. He loves his good albeit ridiculous master despite all the hardship that loyalty to him incurs; does not leave him nor stir from his side, but serves him with honest and admiring fealty—even though sometimes he may lie to him at need. All that makes even Sancho Panza worthy of our affection; it rounds out his figure with humanity and lifts it out of the sphere of the merely comic into that of genuine humour.

Certainly Sancho Panza is national in that he represents the attitude of the Spanish people towards the noble madness of chivalry. This is for good or ill his function. Since yesterday I have been pondering the fact. Here is a nation presented with a travesty of tragedy, a *reductio ad absurdum* of its national qualities, which it turns into its most prized classic masterpiece. Gravely, calmly, proudly, it looks as into a mirror at its own *grandezza*, its idealism, its loftly impracticality, its unmarketable high-mindedness—is this not strange? The historical greatness of Spain lies in bygone centuries. In ours it has to struggle with problems of adaptation. But as for me, what interests me is precisely the difference between what we pompously call history and our own inward, human history. Freedom, light-hearted self-criticism, probably do not ensure a people a prominent role in history. But they give it charm; and, after all, in the end even charm and its opposite play their roles in history. Whatever pessimistic historians may say, human beings have a conscience, even if only an æsthetic one, a feeling for good taste. They bow, of course, before success, before the *fait accompli* of brute force, even of successful crime. But at bottom they do not lose sight of the humanly beautiful, the violently wrong and brutalizing, which has happened in their midst; and in the end without their sympathy might and brute force can reap no lasting success. History is ordinary reality, to which one is born, to which one must be adequate. Upon it Don Quixote's inept loftiness of soul suffers shipwreck. That is winning, and ridiculous. But what would a Don Quixote at the other extreme be like? Anti-idealistic, sinister, a pessimistic believer in force—and yet a Don Quixote? A brutalized Don Quixote? Even Cervantes, with all his melancholic humour, had not gone so far as to concieve that.

May twenty-first. Chair on the promenade deck, plaid and mantle. The fog-horn has been going almost all the time since yesterday evening and most of the night too, I should say; now, this morning, its warning note sounds afresh. It is raining a little, the horizon, our daily infinity, is shrouded in grey, our speed has slowed down. It is windy too. But the sea is smooth as ever, and so we must not speak of bad weather.

Posted on the blackboard is a notice in English to the effect that passengers should assemble with their tickets at eleven o'clock at the numbered boat stations to receive instruction from the appointed emergency officers. I did not see whether others obeyed the order; but we, at least, after the bouillon, which is handed round at this hour by white-jacketed stewards, betook ourselves to the rendezvous. Despite all the thick coating of luxury, which makes one tend to forget the seriousness of things, this idea of an emergency appealed to me. As we went, not quite certain of our goal, we encountered the head steward, well known to us in the dining-room, and learned that he and no other was the captain of our life-boat, our instructor and deliverer. He is a jovial Dutchman, who speaks English and German with the same whimsical turn and glib inadequacy, very much of a good fellow on the surface, but with a calculating eye. He is clean-shaven, with glasses on a slightly hooked nose such as we are used to among the Swabians, in our country. He wears a coat with gold braid, in the evening it is short and cut like a dinner jacket. He led us to the emergency rendezvous, a spot on the open promenade deck, and in his pleasant, droll, guttural, and at the same time rather harsh Hollands German—quite offhand and easy he was—he explained to us the procedure of taking to the boats. Nothing more calculated to inspire confidence. The motor-boat comes down from the upper deck, very nice, only somewhat small for a high sea. It hangs there close to the railings, we get in, they lower it down to the water. Our officer says: "So, now I will take you home."

Home. Curious way to put it, as though riding there upon the waves we were to tell him our address and he would convey us thither in the motor-boat. And home: what does that mean, anyhow? Does it mean Kussnacht near Zürich, where I have lived for a year and am more of a guest than at home, so that I cannot regard it as a proper goal for a life-boat? Does it mean further back, my house in Herzogpark, Munich, where I thought to end my days and which has now revealed itself as nothing but a temporary refuge and *pied-à-terre*? Home—that must mean even further back, to my childhood home, the parental house at *Lübeck*, which still stands at present and yet is so deep-sunken into the past? What a strange captain you are, with your glasses and your golden triangle on your sleeve and your vague assurance about taking us "home"!

Well, at least we are now instructed; we chatted a little while with our guardian angel, for I wanted to know, in particular, whether he had already experienced the emergency and taken to the boats. "Three times," said he. Three times in his professional career had he done it—for a person who went to sea as much as he did it was scarcely avoidable. But how? How had it happened? "You run into something," he said, with mock surprise. You run into something, how else?—that was always happening when one went to sea. We could not imagine it, nor understand how the accredited arts of navigation, in which we blindly confide, should so easily and often miss fire, so that at any moment you might "run into something." But we could get nothing more definite from him. His meagre and glibly employed vocabulary prevented him. Perhaps it was just empty nothings he was telling us, like the fantastic and dreamlike phrase about taking us "home."

In the dining-room this head steward of ours is by preference at the service of those who are well provided with the world's goods. The American family constantly order outside the menu card, regaling themselves on lobster, champagne, omelets, and so on. The head steward moves from table to table, his hands behind his back, smiling with a shallow professional smile behind his glasses, bestowing a little of his joviality upon each. But at the American table he stops a long time, supervises the extra orders, or even lends a helping hand. We can contemplate all this prosperity with the greater detachment in that nobody suffers from it. The entire service is luxurious to the nth degree. It is not confined to a fixed menu; the whole crowded card, fresh every day, is at your disposal and you can put together your meal as you like. If you wanted to you could eat the whole thing from top to bottom every day, from hors d'œuvres to ice-creams. But how soon does man reach his limits! The management is well aware of the fact, and no doubt its principle of choice has proved itself economical, especially in the winter-time.

We sit at the round middle table with two officers: the young and attractive ship's doctor, an American, and the purser, a Dutchman of classic phlegm, and such an appetite that he always gets double portions. Then there is a good-natured little business man from Philadelphia who likes champagne, and in bearing and mentality seems to resemble our merchant type at home. Finally there is an elderly spinster dressed with bourgeois care and laughing a great deal out of pure friendliness. She has been visiting relatives in Holland and is on the way homewards. After landing she must cross a whole continent to get there, for she lives in the state of Washington, on the Pacific coast.

What journeys—many of them so senseless! My wife is beside herself over some twins from Rotterdam, whom we often meet on deck in their carriage. They are being taken on a visit to their grandmother in South Carolina. The old lady wants to see her grandchildren. Well and good. But it is frightfully egotistic, for South Carolina lies farther south than Sicily, in June the climate is insupportable, and if the Rotterdam babies get summer complaint, what will their self-willed grandmother say then? It is no affair of ours; but when one shares the same horizon with such proceedings, one has one's thoughts.

The babies' nurse is Jewish and reads modern books. Their mother eats with the elder brothers and sisters near us, in a corner of the room. All the occupants of the saloon are long since familiar to us. They are few, always the same. Nobody gets in or out—though despite the whimsicality of the thought I catch myself expecting a new face. There is a table of young Dutchmen, obviously on pleasure bent. They burst out in frequent guffaws. At the captain's table, in company with him, sits a distinguished American couple of advanced years. At tea-time this couple sit up very straight in a corner of the music room and read. They complete the list of passengers save for the Jonah of the boat, a raw-boned Yankee whose lips stick out in the Anglo-Saxon fish mouth, under which and not under the chin the English policemen wear their chin straps. He is a man in the middle of the thirties, who has a table all to himself and reads a book while he eats. He has no contact with anyone in the first class. But we see him in "tourist" playing shuffleboard with the Jewish exiles. His aloofness is offensive, he is not liked. Repeatedly I see him making notes in a notebook, in his desk-chair as well as at table. Everybody feels there is something wrong about it all. Who shuts himself off like this and then goes for entertainment to "tourist"? He must be a writer, aloof from the regular order of society and critical of it—but then his evening dress is quite correct. I a little envy him his singleness of purpose about the table and am rather jealous of the Jewish refugees whom he considers worthy of his society. My pride says to me that I am probably capable as they of following the trains of thought he confides to his notebook—though I admit that my interest in him is at present less social than æsthetic and psychological.

I have diverted myself the whole day with the epic wit of Cervantes, in making the adventures of the second part, or at least some of them, grow out of Don Quixote's literary fame, out of the popularity that he and Sancho enjoy, thanks to the earlier part, "their novel," the great history wherein they were first portrayed. They would never have got so far as the ducal court if the distinguished persons there had not known the extraordinary pair so well from reading about them and been enchanted to see them in the flesh and amuse themselves by giving them entertainment. That is new, and unique. I know nowhere else in literature where the hero of a novel lives on his own fame, as it were upon the reputation of his reputation. The simple reappearance of well-known characters in novel sequences, as in Balzac, is after all something quite different. Their existence is confirmed, their personalities achieve greater depth by virtue of our old acquaintance with them and the fact that they were there before and have come back. But they do not change their level; the order of illusion to which they belong remains the same. In Cervantes it is more than this: a sort of romantic illusion, a trick with an ironic undertone. Don Quixote and his squire, in this second part, quit the sphere of reality where they belonged, the novel where they first had their being, to move in person, as more lively realities, through a world which paid them joyous homage. And that world, in its turn, represents a higher stage of reality, although even it is a depicted world, the illusional evocation of a fictive past. Sancho Panza, in the presence of the Duchess, permits himself to jest: "That squire of his, who is, or ought to be, in the same history, called Sancho Panza, that am I, unless I was changed in the cradle, I mean in the press." Yes, Cervantes even evokes a figure out of the detested false sequel, and makes it convict itself out of its own mouth and show that the Don Quixote created by the same author cannot possibly be the right and true one. These are devices after the heart of E. T. A. Hoffmann himself. Indeed, they may be a clue to the source of much in the writers of the romantic school. It cannot be said that they were the greatest artists. But they have thought the most fruitfully about the weird depths, the trick mirrors and false bottoms of artistic illusion; and it is precisely because they were artists in and beyond art that they came so dangerously near to the ironic dissolution of form. It is well to be constantly aware that this is the intimate pitfall of every technique that seeks to combine the humorous with the realistic. From the comic touch of certain epic means of producing reality to the word-plays and artifices of downright buffoonery, faithful to form and yet amorphous, it is only a step. I do indeed give my reader an unexpected opportunity of seeing with his own eyes Joseph, son of Jacob, sitting by the well in the moonlight, and of comparing his bodily presence, fascinating if also humanly incomplete as it is, with the ideal renown that centuries have woven about his figure. But I hope that the humour of this method of seizing the occasion to evoke reality may still deserve the honourable name of art.

May twenty-second. So there goes on, with unresting engines, day by day our steady forward push across the great spaces of the ocean. In my bath in the morning, in the warm, sticky, faintly rotten-smelling sea-water, which impregnates my skin with salt and which I dearly love, I remind myself pleasantly that while we slept we have unrolled another large instalment of the endless perspective. The weather is trying to clear up; there is blue sky in sight, beautifying the water with gleams of southern colour. But soon the warmer light has faded again.

We like to stand towards evening on the boat deck with our faces to the wind, watching our course westwards across the ocean's curve. Always we go toward the setting sun, and our path diverges only the slightest; yesterday we steered straight into the sun, today we are deflected somewhat southwards. The course of a ship like ours through the reaches of water is proud and beautiful; as movement certainly more dignified than the roaring of a train round a curve. The absolute void before us is very striking—on a "stretch" followed by the ships of all seagoing countries. We are now in our fourth day, and so far we have not seen the smoke of a single steamer. The explanation is simple: there is too much room. The spaciousness has something cosmic; no matter how many ships, they lose themselves in it like stars in the sky, and only occasionally does one meet another.

Daily the blackboard warns us to set back our watches, from half an hour to forty minutes—yesterday it was thirty-nine. Officially this happens at midnight, but we perform the significant little act soon after dinner, in order that the night may be not all too long, the evening longer. Thus during music and reading do we relive a space in time, which we have already once passed through. It gives us to think, this setting the minute-hand to traverse a segment of time-path for the third time in a day. Ten times thirty-nine minutes is six and a half hours, which we lose—no, gain—on this voyage. Are we then going back in time whilst we press forward in space? Certainly, since our journey is westwards, against the motion of the globe. The word "cosmic," which I used before, is the only one adequate to the situation. World-space and world-time conceptions are pertinent, forcing themselves upon the consciousness despite all this superficial comfort, which makes light of the elements and seeks to rob them of their life-and-death character. We are coming into strange days, into regions of the earth's surface that turn round the sun otherwise than those where we have yet dwelt; where it will still be night and we still sleeping when it is bright daylight at home. All this is common knowledge. Yet I debate it with myself afresh. If we were to keep on travelling westwards, so that we returned via the farthest East, we should gain time all the way to the extent of a whole day and a breach in the calendar, and then slowly lose it again till we were where we were before. The same is true in our present case, when we shall not go all the way round but only back to our own continent. And no harm done. For we do not gain a day of life with a day of time. If we should try to impose upon the cosmic order and, having arrived over there, went neither forwards nor back but brooded over our six hours, guarding them as Fafner his hoard, the portion of life organically assigned to us would not be by one second increased.

What naïve reflections! And, after all, has not the cosmological view of the universe, by comparison with its opposite, the psychological, something puerile about it? As I write I think of Albert Einstein's bright round eyes, like a child's. I cannot help it. Human knowledge, research into human life, has a riper, more mature character than speculations about the Milky Way—with the profoundest respect I say it. Goethe says: "The individual is free to busy himself with whatever attracts and pleasures him, whatever seems to him of worth; but the true study of mankind is man!"

As for *Don Quixote*, it is indeed a strange product: naïve, unique, arbitrary and sovereign in its contradictions. I cannot but shake my head over the single tales scattered through it, so extravagantly sentimental they are, so precisely in the style and taste of the very productions that the poet had set himself to mock. He crams his hosts of readers full to their hearts' content with the very diet from which he would wean them—a pleasant cure! In those idylls he resigns his earlier role, as though to say that if the age wanted that sort of thing he could give it to them, yes, even be a master at it. But I am not so clear about the position with regard to those humanistic speeches which he sometimes puts in his hero's mouth; whether he does not thereby distort the character, overstep its limits, and inartistically speak for himself. They are excellent, these speeches; for instance, upon education, and upon the poesy of nature and of art, which the knight in the green mantle gets to hear. They are full of pure reason, justice, human benevolence, and nobility of form, so that he in the green mantle is justly astonished, "and indeed so much that he wavered in his earlier opinion that the man must be foolish." Quite rightly so, and the reader should waver too. Don Quixote is a bit cracked but not in the least stupid, though the fact was not so clear, even to the author himself, in the beginning. His respect for the creature of his own comic invention grows during the narrative. This process is perhaps the most fascinating thing in the whole novel; it is a novel in itself, waxing proportionately with his regard for his work, which at first he conceived modestly, as a pretty crude and downright satire, without a notion of the extent to which his hero was destined to grow in stature, symbolically and humanly. The change in the point of view permits and even causes a considerable identification of the author with his hero, an inclination to assimilate his intellectual attainments to the author's own, to make him the mouthpiece of Cervantes's convictions and to heighten by cultural and intellectual gifts the picturesque charm which, despite his doleful exterior, his own mad idea develops in Don Quixote. It is his master's elegance of thought and diction that is often the source of Sancho's boundless admiration—and he is not the only one to be fascinated by it.

May twenty-third. Less motion; the weather is warmer. The milder and moister airs of the Gulf Stream prevail.

I begin the day with a fifteen-minute game of medicine ball with a steward from Hamburg, up on the boat deck. He is a reader of mine, he says. After that I breakfast, starting with half a grapefruit, that refreshing large orange of which there is apparently an inexhaustible supply on board. For our greater ease and enjoyment the pulp is loosened from the skin in the kitchen with a special instrument. On the other hand I have not succeeded in making friends with the tomato cocktail which Americans drink down before every meal. It is too sweet.

Since one must get exercise and the everlasting round of the promenade deck becomes a bore, we have taken up deck games and beguile some hours with them both morning and evening. We play shuffleboard in company with a friendly young Dutchman. The red squares full of numbers are painted everywhere on the decks; it is a good and lively game. You have a shovel-shaped stick with which to shoot the round pieces of wood onto a field, or rather into the middle of each field so that they do not touch any of the bounding lines. You must avoid the minus field and try to reach the one marked ten plus; if a piece has got stuck you must improve its lie with your next shot; and finally you must cannon your opponent out of the good positions. All which is easier said than done, and not made less difficult by the shifting nature of the field, which sways to and fro with the motion of the vessel. The best aim helps but little, for the pieces move apparently at random, guided by incalculable powers. Your vexation reinforces your exercise to the point of making you presently deserve and require a hearty meal.

A more complex game than shuffleboard is deck golf, played on a miniature artificial turf, otherwise a flat, green-covered platform. You are supposed to propel the light balls with bats from a cluster of six close-lying openings through one narrow door into the hole at the other end of the course—naturally in the fewest possible strokes. Theoretically one would be able, at least from one of the centre positions, to get through the gate and into the hole at a single shot. But who succeeds in doing it? Three shots make an honourable, two a brilliant record. Usually there are the worst sort of miscarriages and ricochetings, and then you meekly write up a six or seven on the blackboard.

For the tea-hour and after dinner we mostly sit in the blue salon, called the social hall, and listen to the music. Sometimes, especially in the afternoon, we are the only audience. For our sake, although we could do without it, the musicians play; but somebody must be present or they do not play. Sometimes, looking through the windows from the outside, we see the "unemployed" lounging dully at their music-stands. But if a single guest enters the hall, they seize their instruments and begin. The orchestra consists of piano, two violins, viola, and cello. The first violin conducts. The programs, naturally, are very light. A potpourri from *Carmen*, a *Traviata* fantasy, these are the "high spots." Commonly—that is probably the right word—they are all sugary pieces for the tea-hour. The more ambitious ones are all after Puccini, which delights civilized normal man the world over. So they serve it up even here in the midst of space, that he may feel himself well wadded by the usual and getting his money's worth. On such a voyage everything depends upon unconsciousness, upon sustaining a forgetful attitude of mind. But while the hackneyed music is doing its best I sometimes out of sheer native rebelliousness gaze out at the window of the social hall and again through the window of the promenade deck outside at the grey-green, foam-tossed wilderness, at the horizon, which rises, hangs poised for a few seconds, and then sinks again.

We applaud the musicians and they thank us through the first violin, apparently surprised and pleased each time. But they have their independent joy in their work as well; exchange glances at this or that place, discuss the rendering, and laugh among themselves. I look at them and reflect that we should be careful not to judge these men too lightly. There they sit and fiddle away sweet nothings. It is their job. But we have proof and precedent that they can sit like that and play *Nearer, My God, to Thee* up to the very last minute. . . . One must think of them in this light too.

At odd times I read in my orange-coloured volumes and am appalled at Cervantes's intemperate cruelty. For despite that considerable assimilation of the hero to his creator, of which I wrote yesterday, despite the author's high respect for the work of his brain, his inventiveness runs riot in ridiculous and humiliating pitfalls, into which the high-minded hero then tumbles and most comically disgraces himself—as in the adventure with the cheeses, which the "low-minded" Sancho Panza put into Don Quixote's helmet and which began to melt at the moment of high pathos and send streams of curd over the knight's eyes and beard, so that he thinks his brains are softening or he is sweating some horrible sort of sweat—whereat he forfends the thought that it might be a sweat of fear. There is something sardonic and desperately funny in such inventions—as, for another instance, that about the wooden cage in which Don Quixote was "cooped up" and dragged about. Humiliation could not further go. He gets endless beatings, almost as many as Lucious in the story of the Ass. And yet his creator loves and honours him. Does not all this cruelty look like self-flagellation, self-revilement, castigation? Yes, it seems to me as though here the author abandons to scorn his oft-flouted belief in the idea, in the human being and his ennoblement; that this grim coming to terms with reality is actually the definition of humour.

Cervantes puts into Don Quixote's mouth an admirable critique of the nature of translation. It seems to him, he says, that a translation from one language into another is like a Flemish carpet looked at on the wrong side: "for though the figures come out, they are full of threads which mar them and show them not in full beauty and completeness as on the right side. But I will not say that on that account translation is not a praiseworthy work." The metaphor is striking. Only two Spanish translators are exempted, Figueroa and Xauregui. With them one can scarcely distinguish between translation and original. They must have been extraordinary, those two. But in the name of Cervantes I should like to except another name: that of Ludwig Tieck, who in the German *Don Quixote* has made another right side to the carpet.

May twenty-fourth. Yesterday *The Golden Ass* came into my head and ran off my pen—not quite by chance, since I came upon certain affinities between the late-classic novel and *Don Quixote*; though in my ignorance I do not know if others have not found them before. The scenes and episodes I mean become striking by their inherent oddness and lack of motivation, indicating a diffused origin. It is significant that they are in the second, intellectually more ambitious part of the book.

There is, in the first place, in the ninth book, the story of "The Wedding of Camacho, with Other Delightful Incidents." Delightful? Why, this wedding is a frightful affair; but the word as it stands in the chapter-head anticipates the *blague*, the delusion, the secret mockery and farce, the tragic practical joke, which await the reader and most of the characters as well. In the end everything gives place to bewildered laughter. The rustic betrothal feast of the beautiful Quiteria with the rich Camacho is described with florid extravagance. Comacho is the happy rival of the scorned but stout-hearted Basilio, who is only scorned by command, for he has loved his neighbour's daughter Quiteria since childhood and she loves him in turn, so that they really belong together before God and man. The union of the fair one with the rich Comacho happens only by the iron command of the bride's father. The festivities have got as far as the betrothal when amid great outcry the unhappy Basilio appears, "clad in a black jacket, all welted with crimson in flames," and in a trembling voice makes a speech. He says that he, the moral obstacle to the full and undisturbed happiness of the pair, will put himself out of the way. He cries: "'Long live the rich Camacho with the ungrateful Quiteria! Many and happy ages may they live; and let poor Basilio die, whose poverty clipped the wings of his good fortune and laid him in his grave!' So saying, he laid hold of his truncheon, which was stuck in the ground; and drawing out a short tuck that was concealed in it and to which it served as a scabbard; and setting what may be called the hilt upon the ground, with a nimble spring and determined purpose he threw himself upon it and in an instant half the bloody point appears at his back, the poor wretch lying along the ground weltering in his blood and pierced through with his own weapon."

One cannot imagine a more horrid interruption to a gay and splendid feast. Everyone rushes up, Don Quixote himself dismounts from his Rosinante to assist the unhappy wretch, the priest takes charge of him and suffers no one to draw the dagger from the wound before Basilio has confessed, for the drawing out and the death of the victim would be one and the same thing. The devoted one comes a little to himself and in a faint voice expresses the wish that Quiteria might give him her hand as his bride in the last moments of his life, thus extenuating his sinful death. What can he mean? Shall the rich Camacho resign in favour of Death? The priest warns the dying man to think rather upon his own soul and to confess; but Basilio, rolling his eyes and obviously at his last gasp, swears that he will never confess until Quiteria gives him her hand. This, then, a Christian soul being in the balance, comes to pass, with the consent to boot of the pious Camacho. But scarcely has the benediction been pronounced when up springs Basilio most nimbly, draws out the dagger from his body, which had served it for a sheath, and to the bystanders, who are crying out "A miracle, a miracle!" pertly responds: "No miracle, only a stratagem." In short, it turns out that the dagger has not gone through Basilio's ribs, but through a lead pipe filled with blood, all this having been a trick arranged between the lovers. Thanks to the good nature of Camacho and the wise and kindly words of Don Quixote the whole results in Basilio keeping his Quiteria and the resumption of the feasting in honour of the bridal pair.

Is this really fair? The suicide scene is painted with complete seriousness and tragic emphasis. The emotions of horror roused not only in the other actors but in the reader as well are quite unequivocal. Yet in the end the whole thing dissolves in laughter and betrays itself as a farce and travesty. It is not a little annoying. The question is: are such practical mystifications really suitable for art—for art as we understand it? I am instructed by Erwin Rohde and by the excellent book which the mythologist and historian of religion Karl Kerenyi wrote in Budapest on the Greco-Roman novel, that the fabulists of late antiquity had an extraordinary love of such scenes. The Alexandrian novel-writers Achilleus Tatius relates in his *History of Leucippe and Cleitophon* how the heroine is slain horribly by Egyptian swamp robbers. The deed is described in all its barbaric detail. It takes place before the eyes of her beloved, who stands separated from her by a wide ditch, and who then is about to slay himself in despair upon her grave. But now companions appear, whom likewise he had thought dead, draw his beloved safe and sound out of the grave, and relate to him that they too had been captured by the natives; that the sacrifice had devolved upon them and that with the help of a property dagger, with the blade on a spring, and a piece of gut filled with blood they had pretended to carry out the deed. Do I deceive myself, or do this blood-filled gut and the trick dagger in Don Quixote come from the same school?

The second case is reminiscent of Apuleius himself. I mean the highly remarkable adventure of the ass's bray, which is told in the eighth and tenth chapters of Cervantes's ninth book. Two country justices, the ass of one of whom has run away, go together to the mountains where they think the ass is hiding, and since they cannot find it, try to lure it by imitating its bray, an art in which they are marvellously proficient. One stands here, the other there, and they bray against each other; and always when one makes himself heard, the other runs to the spot convinced that the ass is there, because only he could bray so like life. They overwhelm each other with compliments on their remarkable gifts. But the reason why the ass does not come is that he lies in the bushes devoured by wolves. The magistrates find him at length and, hoarse and exhausted, wend their way homewards. The story of the braying contest spreads abroad, so that the people of the village become the mock of all the neighbouring ones. They are put beside themselves by braying from all sides; bitter quarrels, yes, even passages at arms ensue between village and village, and Don Quixote and Sancho Panza march in upon the sally to one of these. For in the usual way the ass-villagers have made of the jest an honour and a watchword: they issue forth with a white satin banner upon which a braying ass is painted, under which emblem they march towards the anti-asses with lances, crossbows, partisans, and halberds to deliver them a battle. But Don Quixote puts himself in the way. He makes a lofty speech, wherein he admonishes them in the name of reason to desist from their purpose and not let it come to bloodshed for such trifles. They seem willing to listen to him. But now Sancho mixes in to clinch the matter and says that not only would it be folly to be angered at sound of a bray, but that also he himself in his youth could bray with such infectious versimilitude that all the asses in the village answered him. And in token that it is an art, which, like swimming, once learned is never forgotten, he holds his nose and brays till all the near-by valleys echo—to his own huge undoing. For the villagers, not being able to bear hearing it, thrash him soundly, and even Don Quixote, quite contrary to his practice, must flee from the threat of their crossbows and partisans. He makes himself scarce; and Sancho, whom, scarcely come to himself, they have "set on his ass" and suffered to follow his master, joins him in flight. Moreover the squadrons, after they have waited the night in vain for the enemy, who have not come out, "returned to their homes joyful and merry" and, adds the scholarly poet, "had they known the practice of the ancient Greeks, they would have erected a trophy in that place."

Extraordinary tale! There are in it associations and affiliations about which I can hardly believe myself mistaken. The ass plays a singular role in the Greco-Roman representational world. He is the animal of Typhon-Set, wicked brother of Osiris; he is the Red One. The mythical hatred of him reached so far into the Middle Ages that the rabbinical Biblical commentaries call him Esau, the name of Jacob's brother, the wild ass. The idea of beating is closely and sacramentally bound up with this phallic conception. The phrase "to beat the ass" has a cult-coloration. Whole herds of asses were ritually beaten as they were driven round the city walls. Also there was the pious custom of pushing the Typhon beast off a rock—just the manner of death which Lucius barely escaped after being turned into an ass in the novel of Apuleius: the robbers threaten him with "*katachremnzesthai*."

Moreover he is beaten for braying, just like Sancho Panza, and continues to be beaten all the time that he is an ass—there are fourteen instances. I may add that according to Plutarch the inhabitants of certain villages so hated the voice of the ass that they put trumpeting under a taboo because it sounded like braying. May not the villagers in *Don Quixote* be a reminiscence of these hypersensitive citizens of antiquity?

It is strange to uncover such a primitive mythical inheritance innocently disguised in the Spanish Renaissance poet. Did he get it from direct knowledge of classic Roman literature? Or did the theme come to him by way of Italy, via Boccaccio? Let scholars decide.

It cleared up in the course of the day and we have a blue sky. The sea is violet-hued—is it not Homer's word? Towards midday we saw wonderful banks of cloud, one behind another, hovering over the water lighted up by the sun—milky-white cushions for angels' feet to tread! A bright and dainty vision.

May twenty-fifth. The young doctor has his misgivings about the weather. He concedes that it is beautiful, but so long as we are under the influence of the Gulf Stream there is no trusting it. Meanwhile we enjoy the happy change, the growing warmth which tells us that we are reaching more southerly zones, the azure purity, the smoother gliding over a quieter sea. We spend almost the whole day on the open boat deck, moving between sun and shade. The sun is treacherous. The wind in our faces prevents us from feeling the heat and meanwhile it does its injurious work unperceived.

Last evening there was cinema in the social hall—we do not lack even this gift of civilization, the company sees to that. But under the prevailing circumstances it seemed strange enough. The white screen was stretched across one end of the room, at the other was set up the wonder-apparatus for sight and sound that progress has developed out of the magic lantern of our childhood. We sit in the slightly swaying elegance of the social hall, in our fauteuils, in dinner jackets, at gilded tables. We drink our tea, smoke our cigarettes, and as in any capital or Eldorado on solid ground gaze at the moving and speaking shadows before us. The actors were in no way inferior to the audience. They were quite as elegant and well groomed. In fact, every actor on the screen is always a pattern of well-dressed well-being. It is the first essential and mitigates the distress of the audience over the trials he must go through. Spacious and elegant perspectives, dining-tables laden with crystal services and fruit—the film loves to make a display of wealth and luxury, mirroring the flattered rich, consoling the poor with dreams. This was an American film. It told the story of a business executive with a weakness for art, music, beauty, and romantic passion. He leaves his wife to pursue in Paris his iridescent dream. His mistimed effort suffers a mild shipwreck: the female who embodies his longing becomes the property of a young musician whom he has helped with money and support; the last scene shows him at the telephone announcing his return to his patient wife— perhaps a melancholy but still a tolerable end, for we know that the spacious salons and crystal table-services of his home await him; that even if he has been disappointed, his experience has had a tranquillizing effect.

It was a pity that so few of us witnessed this pleasing and apposite little drama—ten or twelve persons instead of hundreds in the blue and gold social hall of our luxurious liner. The vacant chairs spoke of loss and change, of a social economy already cracking asunder. Not even all of our stout-hearted forty were there. I missed the fish-mouthed, note-taking American. Where was he? Again with the Jewish exiles in "tourist"? An unsettling man. Travels first-class and takes his meals with us in a dinner jacket; but offensively abjures our intellectual diversions and betakes himself to a foreign, a hostile sphere. People ought to know where they belong. People ought to keep together.

The adventure with the lion is certainly the climax of Don Quixote's "exploits" and in all seriousness the climax of the novel. It is a glorious tale, told with a comic pathos, a sympathetic humour, which betray the poet's genuine enthusiasm for his hero's folly. I read it twice over and was utterly absorbed in its peculiarly moving, magnificently ridiculous contents. The meeting with the pennanted car in which are the African animals, "which the general of Oran was sending to court as a present to His Majesty," is charming as a cultural record. It is evidence of his extraordinary art that after all we have already read of Don Quixote's blind, ill-directed intrepidity, the author can keep us in breathless suspense throughout this adventure. To the horror of his companions and deaf to any reasonable objections, the knight insists that the keeper should let one of the ferocious and hungry animals out of the cage to do battle with him. It is remarkable how Cervantes can sustain a single motive and keep it fresh and effective throughout. Don Quixote's foolhardiness is so astonishing just because he is by no means so mad as not to be aware of it. "Encountering the lions," he says later, "was my unavoidable task, though I knew it to be most extravagant rashness, for I was very well aware that fortitude is a virtue placed between the two vicious extremes of cowardice and foolhardiness. But it is better the valiant should rise to the high pitch of temerity than sink to the low point of cowardice. For as it is easier for the prodigal to become liberal than for the covetous, just so it is much easier for the rash to hit upon being truly valiant than for the coward to rise to true valour." What moral intelligence! The observation of the man in the green mantle is most pertinent: "What he said was coherent, elegant, and well said; what he did was extravagant, rash, and foolish." One almost gets the impression that the author put it forward as a natural and unavoidable antinomy of the higher life.

The classic scene, depicted a hundred times in pictures, where the lean hidalgo dismounts from his mare, fearful lest her courage may not equal his own, and with his trumpery shield and sword, ready for the absurdest duel ever imagined, stands before the open cage full of heroic impatience to get to grips with his enemy—this extraordinary scene lives actually before me in the words of Cervantes. So does the issue of it, which ever so mildly stultifies the knight's heroics. For the king of beasts will not let himself in for such tricks and gambols. He gives one glance, then simply turns his rear foremost and lies unfeelingly down on the floor of his cage. Once more heroics have prosaically missed fire. The whole burden of the theme, all the scorn and mockery of its intent, come down upon Don Quixote's head in the contemptuous, indifferent behavior of the royal beast. The knight is beside himself. He demands of the quaking keeper that he should beat the lion to rouse him to combat. But the man refuses, and at length makes the knight comprehend that he has already displayed the greatness of his courage. No warrior, however doughty, is bound to do more than to challenge his opponent and await him in the open field. If the latter flinches, the blame falls upon him and upon no one else. Don Quixote is finally satisfied. In token of his victory he puts upon his spear the same handkerchief with which he has wiped off his cheesy sweat—whereupon Sancho, who had run away, seeing it from the distance, says: "May I be hanged if my master has not vanquished the wild beasts, for there he summons us." It is a marvel.

In no other place comes out so strongly as here the author's utter readiness to exalt and to abase his hero. But abasement and exaltation are a twin conception the essence of which is distinctly Christian. Their psychological union, their marriage in a comic medium, shows how very much Don Quixote is a product of Christian culture, Christian doctrine, and Christian humanity. It shows as well what Christianity everlastingly means for the world of the mind and of poesy and for the human essence itself and its bold expansion and liberation. I have in mind my Jacob, who whimpered in the dust before the boy Eliphaz, dishonoured to the uttermost, and then, in a dream, out of the very depth of his abased soul produced his great exaltation. Say what you will: Christianity, the flower of Judaism, remains one of the two pillars upon which Western culture rests, the other being Mediterranean antiquity. The denial of one of these fundamental premises of our civilization and education—how much more of both of them—by any group of our European community, would mean its break with that community and an inconceivable, impossible diminishment of its human stature, who knows to what extent? The hectic attack of Nietzsche, the admirer of Pascal, upon Christianity was an unnatural eccentricity; it has always puzzled me, like much else in the character of that tragic hero.

Goethe, more happily balanced and physically less hampered, did not allow his supposed paganism to prevent him from paying homage to Christianity and speaking out for it as the civilizing force that it is. Agitated times like ours always tend to confound the merely epochal with the eternal—as for instance liberalism with freedom—and to throw out the baby with the bath. Thus each free and thoughtful person, each mind which does not flicker in the wind of time, is forced back upon the foundations; driven to become once more conscious of them and to base more solidly upon them. The critique of the twentieth century upon Christian ethic (not to speak of dogma and mythology); the changes that come about naturally with the flow of life; no matter how deep these go, or how transformingly they work, they are and will remain superficial effects. They can never touch the binding authority of the cultural Christianity of the Western world, which once achieved cannot be alienated.

May twenty-sixth. Our newspaper is a very silly sheet, I must confess. It appears daily except Sundays; we need not lack for fresh print any more than for fresh bread. They shove the papers through the slot in our door, where we find them and pick them up when we come down before luncheon. We read them on the spot, for who knows what Europe will do once our backs are turned? Most of the sheet—that is, the advertisements and pictures—is printed beforehand and so possesses no immediacy. But our boat is also provided with wireless: seemingly so alone and forsaken upon the waste of waters, we are in contact with the whole world, can send out messages to every quarter and receive them in turn. Thus what flashes to us from all the continents is printed in the "stop-press" of our news sheet. What did we read today? In the zoological garden of a Western state an ailing tiger was given whiskey as medicine. The ravening beast conceived such a taste for strong drink that he would not give it up when he was cured but now daily demands his dram. That and other such matter we read in our ship's paper. Certainly this particular item is gratifying to read. Not in vain have our news-purveyors reckoned upon our sympathy with the spirit-loving animal. But yet: is there not something like an abuse here? A technical miracle like radio-telegraphy used to transmit such a kind of news over land and sea—ah, humanity, your mental and spiritual development has not kept pace with your technical, it has stopped far behind. Herein lies your lack of faith that your future can be more happy than your past. The gap between your technical maturity and your other unripeness creates precisely the unsatisfied craving with which you clutch at every sheet of news. And so we read of the hilarious tiger. We may be glad that it is no worse. But, after all, the case is the same with our frivolous radio as with our ship's musicians. Under certain circumstances it can send out S O S too. In the name of and for the dignity of technique one might almost wish that it might come to that!

Last evening the wind came up and the ship tossed a good deal in the night. But today we have fine weather again and summery warmth as well. We saw a large fish, like a dolphin, leap high out of the water. There is a report, doubtless false, that we have run over a whale. People repeat it, as a fitting and natural fillip to the voyage. But the bar steward did show us a flight of gulls rocking on the water a little way from the ship, a sign that land is not far off.

And still the day and hour of our arrival remain uncertain. We hear that with a favouring sea and good weather we shall land day after tomorrow in the course of the afternoon. But on the other hand there is the view that we had too much fog at first, that we are behind time and it will be Tuesday before we arrive in the Hudson. This uncertainty constitutes another difference— advantage, I had almost said—from travel by train. Despite all its comfort the sea voyage preserves something primitive. We are given to the incalculable element, we are subject to the inaccuracies of chance—and we like it. But why? In plain terms, because we can thus assert our impatience with mechanical civilization, our craving to reject and deny it as deadly for our souls and our lives? Because we can thus seek and affirm a form of existence that would be nearer the primitive, elemental, uncertain, risky, improvised as in war-time? But am I here voicing the ever growing love of the irrational—that cult for which my critical sense should be ever on the alert, since it is dangerous to humanity and fraught with abuse? My European sympathy for order and reason has made me resist it—more for the sake of equilibrium than because the danger was not present within myself as well. As a teller of tales I have reached the stage of the myth: I would humanize it, would seek, in my unlimited contempt for the soulfully and wilfully barbaric, a rapprochement between humanity and the myth. For I find therein more hope for the future of humanity than in a one-sided struggle against the spirit, time-seeking and enslaved to time, zealously trampling upon reason and civilization. To be able to look into the future one must indeed be of the time. But not only in the sense of actual movement, in which every donkey partakes, bursting with pride and scorn against liberal reactionaries of a different stripe. One must have one's time in oneself entire: not only the revolutionary period, especially when the revolutionary slogan is "Back to the ichthyosaurus!"—but time itself, in all its complexity and contradictoriness; for not one single thing, but many and manifold prefigure the future.

Very arresting and significant is the episode of the Morisco Ricote, the former shopkeeper from Sancho's village, who has been banished from Spain by the Edicts and slips back in pilgrim's garb, urged by homesickness but also in hopes of digging up a buried treasure. The chapter is a shrewd mixture of professions of loyalty and of the author's strict adherence to the church, his blameless submission to the great Philip III—and the most lively human sympathy for the awful fate of the Moorish people, who, attacked by the Edicts of the King, are sacrificed to the supposed interests of the state and driven into misery without regard for individual agony. Through the one position the author purchases immunity for the other; but I suspect, and it has always been felt, that the first was the political means to the second and that the sincerity of the author begins only there. He puts into the mouth of the unhappy Morisco himself an acceptance of His Majesty's commands, an acknowledgment that they spring from indisputable right. Many, he says, had not wanted to believe that the order was seriously meant and considered it a mere threat. But he saw at once that it was an actual law and as such would be put into execution at the appointed time. And what confirmed him in the belief was that he knew of the mischievous extravagant designs "which were such that in my opinion it was a divine inspiration that moved His Majesty to put so brave a resolution into practice." The shameful plots that justify the royal inspiration are not mentioned by name, they remain shrouded in darkness. But not all were guilty. "Some of us," says Ricote, "were steady and true Christian, but these were so few . . . and it is not prudent to nourish a serpent in one's bosom or to keep one's enemies within one's own door." The objectivity and moderation which the author puts in the mouth of the sufferer are most admirable. But gradually and insensibly they are diverted into quite another channel. The Moor says that the punishment was just, a soft and mild one in the opinion of some, but in reality the most terrible that could be inflicted. "Wherever we are we weep for Spain, for in short here were we born and this is our native country. We nowhere find the reception which our misfortune requires. Even in Barbary, and in all other parts of Africa where we expected to be received, cherished, and made much of, there it is we are most neglected and misused." Thus the Spanish Moor continues to mourn, so bitterly that it goes to the heart. "We knew not," he says, "our happiness till we lost it; and so great is the desire almost all of us have to return to Spain that we forsake wife and children and come back again at risk of our lives, so mighty is the love we bear it. And it is now I know, and find by experience, the truth of that common saying: 'Sweet is the love of one's country.'"

Such words as these, the expression of ineradicable natural affinity, obviously give the lie to the phrases about the snake in the bosom, the enemy in the house, the inspired justice of the Edicts, and so forth. The artist's dilemma, expressed in Ricote's speech in the second part of *Don Quixote,* speaks a more convincing language than his careful, obsequious tongue. He sympathizes with the persecuted and banned. They are as good Spaniards as himself or anybody; Spain is their true mother-land; she will not be purer, only poorer, after they have gone, while, once torn from her soil, they are everywhere foreign. Everywhere the words "at home" will be on their lips: "at home in Spain it was thus and thus"—that is, better than where they are. Cervantes, a poor and dependent writer, had all too much need to prove his loyalty; but after he has denied his heart and its honest convictions for only a few moments, he cleanses it again, better than Spain, with all her edicts, can cleanse herself. He condemns the cruelty of the decree that he has just approved—not directly, but by stressing the love of the exiles for their homeland. He even takes it on himself to speak of the freedom of conscience; for Ricote tells how he went from Italy to Germany and there found a sort of peace. For Germany was a good, tolerant country, "its people not standing much upon niceties and everybody living as he pleased, for in most parts of it there is liberty of conscience." Here it was my turn to feel patriotic pride, let the words be old which awake it in me. It is always pleasant to hear praise of home out of a stranger's mouth.

May twenty-seventh. The weather changes quickly at the seashore, but still more quickly and capriciously at sea, where the meteorological variations join forces with our progress and change of sky. Yesterday's summery warmth passed by evening into an overcast sky and an unseasonable sultriness, heavier, damper, and stickier than I have ever experienced. It harassed the nerves like a portent of storm or of some catastrophe. My evening clothes were a burden, I sat bathed in sweat under my stiff shirt, and especially the tea made me burst out in moisture. I do not know how far into the night it held, but today there is a complete change. The forenoon was cool and rainy, a fog came up and the fog-horn went for hours. But suddenly all that disappeared again. The wind changed, the fog lifted, the sky cleared, but despite the sunshine it remained—at least by comparison with the tropic evening of yesterday—so cold that one needed an overcoat and a rug to sit on deck.

A certain excitement makes itself felt. Today is Sunday. In the night, between tomorrow and the day after, they say, we shall get in, lie to in the bay, and land on Tuesday morning at seven.

I must return to what I wrote yesterday and make clear to myself how Cervantes's allegiance as Christian and loyal subject enhances the spiritual values of his freedom, the worth of his criticism. What concerns me is the relativity of all freedom; the fact that it needs to be conditioned and checked, not only outwardly but inwardly as well, in order that it may attain to spiritual worth and be expressive of a higher form of life. It is hard for us to imagine the state of feudal dependence in which artists of former times lived, before that emancipation of the artist ego which has come in with the bourgeois age. One may say that only in very rare cases has this latter been beneficial to the artist as a type. Once the guild of artists modestly based itself on its sense of craftsmanship. It was the fundamental constitution even of the greatest, even of that accidental genius who from time to time got so far as to bow before sovereigns and flower into supernal worth. The whole conception was probably more conducive to the sanity of the artist than are the present ones. In our day we *begin* with emancipation, with the ego, liberty, self-government. Modest simplicity is no longer the nourishing soil of greatness. Once, a given painter or sculptor, thinking to dedicate himself to the calling of beautifying and adorning the world, went as apprentice to a good master; washed brushes, ground colours, rose from the ranks. He became a useful help, to whom the old man doubtless left some work to do, just as the head surgeon at the end of an operation says to his assistant: "You finish!" Finally he himself became, if all went well, a master in his calling— and that was the height of his desire. He was called "*artista*" and the word covered both conceptions, that of artist and craftsman. Even today in Italy every master of a trade is so called. The genius, the great ego, the lonely adventurer, was an exception produced out of the modest, solid, objectively skilled cult of the craft; he achieved royal rank, yet even so he remained a dutiful son of the church and received from her his orders and his material. Today, as I said, we begin with the genius, the ego, the solitary—which is probably morbid. Hugo von Hofmannsthal, who, thanks to his Italo-Austrian origins, had much intuitive sympathy with the eighteenth century, once talked to me amusingly and wittily about the pathetic changes that had taken place in the musician's contacts with life. He said that in former days if you visited a musician he talked something like this: "Do sit down, have a cup of coffee, shall I play to you?" Today, he said, they all sit there like ailing eagles. Precisely. Artists have become ailing eagles because art has become solemn. It elevates and dejects the average artist, with unhappy results; it has made art solitary, melancholy, isolated, misunderstood, turned it, in short, into an ailing eagle.

It is certainly true that the poet represents an art world different from the graphic, the plastic, or the musical. Poetic and literary creation have a special place among the arts since in them the mechanical plays a smaller, in any case a different, role, more immaterial, more mental. On the whole its relation to the mind is more immediate. The poet is not artist alone; or rather he is artist in another, more intellectual way, since his medium is the word, his tool of the mind. But even with him it were desirable that liberty and emancipation stood at the end and not at the beginning, so that as a human being the artist would emerge from modesty, limitation, restraint, independence. For, once more, freedom has worth, it confers rank, only when it is won from unfreedom, when it is the process of becoming free. How much more powerful and intellectually significant is Cervantes's human sympathy for the fate of Ricote the Moor, and his indirect criticism of the state's harsh attitude, *after* he has expressed the submission which with him is a matter not of hypocrisy but of actual intellectual conditioning! All the human freedom and dignity, the emancipation of the artist spirit; the quixotic audacity that mingles cruel humiliation and moving nobility of soul—all this, the genius, independence, and daring, rests upon reverence before the Holy Inquisition, formal devotion to the monarch, acceptance of the protection of great men and their "well-known generosity," for example Count Lenos and Don Bernardo de Sandoval y Roxas. It soars up from these loyal limitations as involuntarily and unexpectedly as the work itself grows out of an entertaining, jesting satire—as which it was conceived—and into a monument of universal literature and symbol of humanity. I take it for a rule that the greatest works were those of the most modest purpose. Ambition may not stand at the beginning; it must not come before the work but must grow with the work, which will itself be greater than the blithely astonished artist dreamed; it must be bound up with the work and not with the ego of the artist. There is nothing falser than abstract and premature ambition, the self-centred pride independent of the work, the pallid ambition of the ego. So possessed, the artist sits there "like an ailing eagle."

May twenty-eighth. Last day on board. Yesterday we met a ship—an experience, for it was the first since we set out. This was a Danish boat, of about our size, with the Dannebrog at her stern. I enjoyed watching the signalled greeting which we engaged, the chivalrous honour that ships everywhere pay each other in passing. A flageolet shrilled from the bridge; and a sailor hastened to haul down our Dutch colours, whilst the Dannebrog sank on the other boat. Then, as we passed, at a second signal the flags went up again and thus seagoing punctilio was satisfied. How charming is this salute! Seafaring men all over are bound into an international comradery by their distinctive calling, which is everywhere alike and everywhere, despite all modern mechanization, possessed by the spirit of bold adventure. So when they meet upon the wide and wildly moody element to which they are equally sworn, they do each other honour and through them the nations do the same. For ships are national emissaries and outlying territory, and they behave as such—so long as their nations are not at war. But that Denmark and Netherlands will not be. They are small, reasonable countries, dispensed of heroic historicity, whilst the others have at bottom nothing else in their heads but war. Thus the flag salute of the great ones has an uncanny air of propriety which ironically conceals quite other possibilities.

The sky is bright and sunny, the sea lightly crisped; the ship moves quietly, with a long, slow leaning to left and right probably caused by the course we are steering. But the difference in temperature from that of the last evening's sultriness remains astonishing. The night was very cold, the morning rather more than fresh, and even now we sit in the sun with plaid and overcoat.

I am inclined to find the end of Don Quixote a little weak. Death here assumes the character of a fixation against all unwarranted literary exploiting, and thereby itself takes on a literary artificiality that is not very convincing. It is not the same whether a beloved creation dies to the author or whether he *makes* it die, brings about and advertises its death, in order that no one else can make it live again. A literary death born of jealousy. But indeed this very jealousy betrays once more the poet's inner and proudly defensive identification with the eternally distinguished creation of his brain. His feeling is deep; no less sincere in that it expresses itself in jesting literary precautions against extraneous attempts at galvanizing the corpse. The priest demands of the notary a certificate "that Alonzo Quixano the Good, commonly called Don Quixote de la Mancha, has departed this life and died a natural death; and he insisted upon this testimonial lest any other author save only Cid Hamet Benengeli falsely should raise him from the dead and write endless stories of his exploits." Cid Hamet himself, however, evaporates at this juncture and betrays himself as the whimsical pretext he always was. He it is indeed who hangs up his pen by a brass wire upon a spit-rack and charges it to cry out to the presumptuous or wicked historians who would take it down to profane it:

> Beware, ye poet thieves, beware!
> Nor steal a single line;
> For Fate has made this work its care,
> And guaranteed it mine.

Who speaks? Who says "mine"? The pen? No, it is another speaker who utters the last line. "For me alone was Don Quixote born and I for him; he understood how to act and I to write, we were destined for each other, maugre and in despite of the scribbling impostor of Tordesillas who has dared or shall dare with gross and ill-cut ostrich feather to describe the exploits of my valorous knight; a burden too weighty for his shoulders and an enterprise beyond his dull and frigid genius." Well the poet knows what noble and humanly heavy burden he has borne in this history which has lightened the heart of all the world. He did not know it at the beginning, but he knew it. And how strange! At the very end he does not know it either. He forgets it again.

He says: "For my only desire was to bring into public abhorrence the fabulous and absurd histories of knight-errantry which, compared with my true and genuine *Don Quixote*, begin already to totter and will doubtless fall, never to rise again. Farewell." That is a return to the modest satirical parody which was the original intention of a work that grew so much beyond it. The death-bed chapter itself expresses this reversion. For Don Quixote is changed before he dies. The dying man wins—oh, joy!—his sane reason back. He has a long sleep, six hours long, and when he wakes he is by God's mercy mentally healed. His mind is free of the fog that had invaded it by the much reading of those dreadful books of knight-errantry; he sees their senselessness and depravity and will be no longer Don Quixote de la Mancha, knight of the doleful countenance, knight of the lions, but Alonzo Quixano, a reasonable man, a man like other men. That should rejoice us. But it rejoices us strikingly little, it leaves us cold, and to some extent we regret it. We are sorry about Don Quixote—as indeed we were sorry for him when affliction at his defeat stretched him out on his bed of death. For that is actually the cause of his demise; the doctor declares "that melancholy and vexation brought about his death." It is the deep dejection of seeing shipwrecked his mission as knight-errant and light-bringer that killed him. And we, hearing still in our ear that weak and sickly voice speaking the words: "Dulcinea is the most beautiful damsel in the world and I the unhappiest knight, but it is not fitting that my weakness should deny this truth; lay on, knight, with thy lance!"—we share in his defeat, though we know that his mission could not turn out otherwise, being the whimsy and maggot that it was. Even so in the course of the story the whimsy becomes so endeared to us that we are prepared and even eager to let it stand for the spirit, to feel for it as though it were spirit itself—and that we finely owe to the poet.

The case was most difficult. A conflict is present. If the work had only remained true to its original purpose of bringing to scorn the books of knight-errantry, through the ridiculous undertakings and overthrowings of a witless knight, then everything would be simple enough. But since all unexpectedly it expanded so much beyond its fundamental idea, the possibility of a satisfactory ending was destroyed. To let Don Quixote fall and die in one of his senseless enterprises was unthinkable, it would have gone beyond a joke and jarred on Cervantes's audience. To make him live after his return to sanity would not do either; that would be to make the husk survive beyond the soul; would be a degradation of the character below its lofty height—quite aside from the fact that for reasons connected with literary patronage he had to die anyway. I can see that it would have been neither Christian nor edifying to let him die in his delusion, saved indeed from the lance of the knight of the silver moon, but in despair over his downfall. It was needful that his despair be dissipated in his dying hour by the knowledge that it was all madness. But after all is there not death in the revelation that Dulcinea was not an adorable princess but a peasant girl off a dung-hill, and that all his actions, griefs, and aspirations were moonshine? Should he not then curse God and die? Certainly it was imperative to save Don Quixote's soul to sanity before he died. But in order that this salvation might be after our hearts, the author should have made his unreason less lovable.

Thus we see that genius may become an embarrassment, and that it can spoil an author's conception. However, not too much is made of Don Quixote's death. It is the sympathetically imagined passing, dignified and Christlike, of a good man, after he has confessed, received ghostly consolation, and set his earthly affairs in order with the notary. "As all human things, especially the lives of men, are transitory, incessantly declining from their beginning until they arrive at their final period; and as that of Don Quixote had no particular privilege from Heaven, to exempt it from the common fate, his end and dissolution came when he least thought of it." The reader must take that not too seriously, as did the friends whom Don Quixote left behind, his housekeeper, his niece, and Sancho, his former squire. These indeed mourned him with all their heart; the reader sees again what a good master he has been; yes, there is the grotesque description of "the sluices of their swollen eyes when the news that he must die forced a torrent of tears from their eyes and a thousand groans from their hearts." It is easy to give a comic turn to the description of sincere sorrow. "Human nature is human nature," "life must go on," and so forth. . . . We are told that during the three days of Don Quixote's agony, though "the whole house was in confusion, yet the niece ate, the housekeeper drank, and Sancho Panza made much of himself; for this business of legacies effaces, or moderates, the grief that is naturally due to the deceased." A mocking tribute to realism, an unsentimental attitude which may once have caused offence. The stoutest and boldest conqueror in the realm of human nature was always well armed with a sense of humour.

Afternoon, six o'clock. We have packed—which was quite a job, kneeling on the floor beside our trunks. The sense of arrival is pervading the ship. One sees the crew getting ready to stand by the ropes. Our American companions visibly rejoice in the homecoming which to us is the opposite. It is evening. On our right as we move slowly up the bay stretch the lights of Long Island, whose beaches and country estates we have heard celebrated. We go early to bed, tomorrow we rise early. To be ready is all.

May twenty-ninth. The weather is still fine, fresh and slightly misty. Since we took leave at dawn of our beds, where we have rocked so many nights through, the ship, which lay to during the night, so that for the first time we were without the throb of her engines, has slowly got under way. We have breakfasted, given the last touches to our luggage, handed out the final tips. Ready for arrival, we await it on deck. Through the mist rises a familiar figure, the Goddess of Liberty with her crown, a naïve classicistic symbol grown right strange to us today.

I feel dreamy from the early rising and strange experience of this hour. And I dreamed in the night too, in the unfamiliar silence of the engines; now I try to recall the dream which assembled itself from my reading. I dreamed of Don Quixote, it was he himself, and I talked with him. How distinct is reality, when one encounters it, from one's fancy! He looked different from the pictures; he had a thick, bushy moustache, a high retreating forehead, and under the likewise bushy brows almost blind eyes. He called himself not the Knight of the Lions but Zarathustra. He was, now that I had him face to face, very tactful and courteous, so that I recalled with strong emotion the words that I had read about him yesterday: "for in truth, as has been said before, both while he was plain Alonzo Quixano and while he was Don Quixote de la Mancha, he was ever of an amiable disposition and affable behaviour, and was therefore beloved, not only by those of his own family, but by all that knew him."

Pain, love, pity, and boundless reverence filled me altogether as this prescription became real. Dreamily they hover about me in this hour of arrival.

But such thoughts are too European for my surroundings—they face in the wrong direction. Ahead out of the morning mist slowly emerge the skyscrapers of Manhattan, a fantastic landscape group, a towered city of giants.

FRANZ KAFKA

The Truth about Sancho Panza

Sancho Pansa, der sich übrigen dessen nie gerühmt hat, gelang es im Laufe der Jahre, durch Beistellung einer Menge Ritter-und Räuberromane in den Abendund Nachtstunden seinen Teufel, dem er später den Namen Don Quichotte gab, derart von sich abzulenken, dass dieser dann haltlos die verrücktesten Taten aufführte, die aber mangels eines vorbestimmten Gegenstandes, der eben Sancho Pansa hätte sein sollen, niemandem schadeten. Sancho Pansa, ein freier Mann, folgte gleichmütig, vielleicht aud einem gewissen Verantwortlichkeitsgefühl, dem Don Quichotte auf seinen Zügen und hatte davon eine grosse und nützliche Unterhaltung bis an sein Ende.

Without making any boast of it Sancho Panza succeeded in the course of years, by devouring a great number of romances of chivalry and adventure in the evening and night hours, in so diverting from him his demon, whom he later called Don Quixote, that his demon thereupon set out in perfect freedom on the maddest exploits, which, however, for the lack of a preordained object, which should have been Sancho Panza himself, harmed nobody. A free man, Sancho Panza philosophically followed Don Quixote on his crusades, perhaps out of a sense of responsibility, and had of them a great and edifying entertainment to the end of his days.

From *Parables*. © 1946, 1947 Schocken Books Inc. Translated by Willa and Edwin Muir.

ERICH AUERBACH

The Enchanted Dulcinea

Yo no veo, Sancho, dijo Don Quijote, sino a tres labradoras sobre tres borricos.

—Ahora me libre Dios del diablo, respondió Sancho; ¿y es posible que tres hacaneas, o como se llaman, blancas como el ampo de la nieve, le parezcan a vuesa merced borricos? Vive el Señor, que me pele estas barbas si tal fuese verdad.

—Pues yo te digo, Sancho amigo, dijo Don Quijote, que es tan verdad que son borricos o borricas, como yo soy Don Quijote, y tú Sancho Panza: a lo menos a mí tales me parecen.

—Calle, señor, dijo Sancho, no diga la tal palabra, sino despabile esos ojos, y venga a hacer reverencia a la señora de sus pensamientos, que ya llega cerca: y diciendo esto se adelantó a recebir a las tres aldeanas, y apeándose del rucio tuvo del cabestro al jumento de una de las tres labradoras, y hincando ambas rodillas en el suelo, dijo:

—Reina y princesa y duquesa de la hermosura, vuestra altivez y grandeza sea servida de recebir en su gracia y buen talante al cautivo caballero vuestro, que allí está hecho piedra mármol, todo turbado y sin pulsos de verse ante vuesa magnífica presencia. Yo soy Sancho su escudero, y él es el asendereado caballero Don Quijote de la Mancha, llamado por otro nombre el Caballero de la Triste Figura.

From *Mimesis: The Representation of Reality in Western Literature.* © 1953 by Princeton University Press.

A esta sazón ya se había puesto Don Quijote de hinojos junto a Sancho, y miraba con ojos desencajados y vista turbada a la que Sancho llamaba reina y señora; y como no descubría en ella sino una moza aldeana y no de muy buen rostro, porque era carirredonda y chata, estaba suspenso y admirabo, sin osar desplegar los labios. Las labradoras estaban asimismo atónitas viendo a aquellos dos hombres tan diferentes hincados de rodillas, que no dejaban pasar adelante a su compañera; pero rompiendo el silencio la detenida, toda desgradiada y mohina, dijo:

—Apártense nora en tal del camino, y dejenmos pasar, que vamos de priesa.

A lo que respondió Sancho:

—Oh princesa y señora universal del Toboso, ¿cómo vuestro magnífico corazón no se enternece viendo arrodillado ante vuestra sublimada presencia a la coluna y sustento de la andante caballería?

Oyendo lo cual otra de las dos dijo:

—Mas yo que te estrego burra de mi suegro: mirad con qué se vienen los señoritos ahora a hacer burlas de las aldeanas, como si aquí no supiésemos echar pullos como ellos: vayan su camino, y déjenmos hacer el nueso, y serles ha sano.

—Levántate, Sancho, dijo a este punto Don Quijote, que ya veo que la fortuna, de mi mal no harta, tiene tomados los caminos todos por donde pueda venir algún contento a esta ánima mezquina que tengo en las carnes. Y tú, oh extremo valor que puede desearse, término de la humana gentileza, único remedio de este afligido corazón que te adora, ya que el maligno encantador me persigue, y ha puesto nubes y cataratas en mis ojos, y para sólo ellos y no para otros ha mudado y transformando tu sin igual hermosura y rostro en el de una labradora pobre, si ya también el mío no le ha cambiado en el de algún vestiglo para hacerle aborrecible a tus ojos, no dejes de mirarme blanda y amorosamente, echando de ver en esta sumisión y arrodillamiento que a tu contrahecha hermosura hago, la humildad con que mi alma te adora.

—Toma que me agüelo, respondió la aldeana, amiguita soy yo de oír resquebrajos. Apártense y déjenmos ir, y agradecérselo hemos.

Apartóse Sancho y déjola ir, contentísimo de haber salido bien de su enredo. Apenas se vió libre la aldeana que había hecho la figura de Dulcinea cuando picando a su hacanea con un aguijón que en un palo traía, dió a correr por el prado adelante; y como la borrica sentía la punta del aguijón, que le fatigaba más de lo ordinario, comenzó a dar corcovos, de manera que dió con la señora Dulcinea en tierra: lo cual visto por Don Quijote, acudió a levantarla, y Sancho a componer y cinchar el albarda, que también vino a la barriga de la pollina. Acomodada pues el albarda, y queriendo Don Quijote

levantar a su encantada señora en los brazos sobre la jumenta, la señora
levantándose del suelo le quitó de aquel trabajo, porque haciéndose algún
tanto atrás tomó una corridica, y puestas ambas manos sobre las ancas de la
pollina dió con su cuerpo más ligero que un halcón sobre la albarda, y quedó
a horcajadas como si fuera hombre, y entonces dijo Sancho:

—¡Vive Roque, que es la señora nuestra ama más ligera que un alcotán,
y que puede enseñar a subir de la jineta al más diestro cordobés o mejicano;
el arzón trasero de la silla pasó de un salto, y sin espuelas hace correr la
hacanea como una cebra, y no le van en zaga sus doncellas, que todas corren
como el viento!

Y así era la verdad, porque en viéndose a caballo Dulcinea todas
picaron tras ella y dispararon a correr, sin volver la cabeza atrás por espacio
de más de media legua. Siguiólas Don Quijote con las vista, y cuando vió que
no parecían, volviéndose a Sancho le dijo:

—Sancho, ¿qué te parece, cuán mal quisto soy de encantadores? . . .

("I see nothing," declared Don Quixote, "except three farm girls on
three jackasses."

"Then God deliver me from the devil!" exclaimed Sancho. "Is it
possible that those three hackneys, or whatever you call them, white as the
driven snow, look like jackasses to your Grace? By the living God, I would
tear out this beard of mine if that were true!"

"But I tell you, friend Sancho, it is as true that those are jackasses, or
she-asses, as it is that I am Don Quixote and you Sancho Panza. At least, that
is the way they look to me."

"Be quiet, sir," Sancho admonished him, "you must not say such a thing
as that. Open those eyes of yours and come do reverence to the lady of your
affections, for she draws near."

Saying this, he rode on to meet the village maids and, slipping down off
his donkey, seized one of their beasts by the halter and fell on his knees in
front of its rider.

"O queen and princess and duchess of beauty," he said, "may your
Highness and Majesty be pleased to receive and show favor to your captive
knight, who stands there as if turned to marble, overwhelmed and breathless
at finding himself in your magnificent presence. I am Sancho Panza, his
squire, and he is the world-weary knight Don Quixote, otherwise known as
the Knight of the Mournful Countenance."

By this time Don Quixote was down on his knees beside Sancho. His
eyes were fairly starting from their sockets and there was a deeply troubled
look in them as he stared up at the one whom Sancho had called queen and
lady; all that he could see in her was a village wench, and not a very pretty

one at that, for she was round-faced and snub-nosed. He was astounded and perplexed and did not dare open his mouth. The girls were also very much astonished to behold these two men, so different in appearance, kneeling in front of one of them so that she could not pass. It was this one who most ungraciously broke the silence.

"Get out of my way," she said peevishly, "and let me pass. And bad luck go with you. For we are in a hurry."

"O princess and universal lady of El Toboso!" cried Sancho. "How can your magnanimous heart fail to melt as you behold kneeling before your sublimated presence the one who is the very pillar and support of knight-errantry?"

Hearing this, one of the others spoke up. "Whoa, there, she-ass of my father!" she said. "Wait until I curry you down. Just look at the small-fry gentry, will you, who've come to make sport of us country girls! Just as if we couldn't give them tit for tat. Be on your way and get out of ours, if you know what's good for you."

"Arise, Sancho," said Don Quixote, "for I perceive that fortune has not had her fill of evil done to me but has taken possession of all the roads by which some happiness may come to what little soul is left within me. And thou, who art all that could be desired, the sum of human gentleness and sole remedy for this afflicted heart that doth adore thee! The malign enchanter who doth persecute me hath placed clouds and cataracts upon my eyes, and for them and them alone hath transformed thy peerless beauty into the face of a lowly peasant maid; and I can only hope that he has not likewise changed my face into that of some monster by way of rendering it abhorrent in thy sight. But for all of that, hesitate not to gaze upon me tenderly and lovingly, beholding in this act of submission as I kneel before thee a tribute to thy metamorphosed beauty from this humbly worshiping heart of mine."

"Just listen to him run on, will you? My grandmother!" cried the lass. "Enough of such gibberish. We'll thank you to let us go our way."

Sancho fell back and let her pass, being very thankful to get out of it so easily.

No sooner did she find herself free than the girl who was supposed to have Dulcinea's face began spurring her "cackney" with a spike on the end of a long stick that she carried with her, whereupon the beast set off at top speed across the meadow. Feeling the prick, which appeared to annoy it more than was ordinarily the case, the ass started cutting such capers that the lady Dulcinea was thrown to the ground. When he saw this, Don Quixote hastened to lift her up while Sancho busied himself with tightening the girths and adjusting the packsaddle, which had slipped down under the animal's belly. This having been accomplished, Don Quixote was about to take his enchanted lady in his arms to place her upon the she-ass when the girl saved him the trouble by jumping up from the ground, stepping back a few paces, and taking a run for it. Placing both hands upon the crupper of the ass, she landed more lightly than a falcon upon the packsaddle and remained sitting there astride it like a man.

"In the name of Roque!" exclaimed Sancho, "our lady is like a lanner, only lighter, and can teach the cleverest Cordovan or Mexican how to mount. She cleared the back of the saddle in one jump, and without any spurs she makes her hackney run like a zebra, and her damsels are not far behind, for they all of them go like the wind."

This was the truth. Seeing Dulcinea in the saddle, the other two prodded their beasts and followed her on the run, without so much as turning their heads to look back for a distance of half a league. Don Quixote stood gazing after them, and when they were no longer visible he turned to Sancho and spoke.

"Sancho," he said, "you can see now, can you not, how the enchanters hate me?") *Don Quixote*, by Miguel de Cervantes Saavedra. Translated by Samuel Putnam. The Viking Press. 1949.

This is a passage from chapter 10 of part 2 of Cervantes' *Don Quijote*. The knight has sent Sancho Panza to the hamlet of El Toboso to call on Dulcinea and announce his intention of paying her a visit. Sancho, entangled in his earlier lies, and not knowing how to find the imaginary lady, decides to deceive his master. He waits outside the hamlet for a time, long enough to make Don Quijote believe that he has done his errand. Then, seeing three peasant women on donkeys riding toward him, he hurries back and tells his master that Dulcinea and two of her ladies are coming to greet him. The knight is overwhelmed with surprise and joy, and Sancho leads him toward the peasant women, describing their beauty and splendid gear in glowing colors. But for once Don Quijote sees nothing except the actual reality, that is, three peasant women on donkeys—and this leads to the scene we have quoted.

Among the many episodes which represent a clash between Don Quijote's illusion and an ordinary reality which contradicts it, this one holds a special place. First because it is concerned with Dulcinea herself, the ideal and incomparable mistress of his heart. This is the climax of his illusion and disillusionment: and although this time too he manages to find a solution, a way to save his illusion, the solution (Dulcinea is under an enchantment) is so intolerable that henceforth all his thoughts are concentrated upon one goal: to save her and break the enchantment. In the last chapters of the book, his recognition or foreboding that he will never achieve this is the direct preparation for his illness, his deliverance from his illusion, and his death. In the second place the scene is distinguished by the fact that here for the first time the roles appear exchanged. Until now it had been Don Quijote who, encountering everyday phenomena, spontaneously saw and transformed them in terms of the romances of chivalry, while Sancho was generally in doubt and often tried to contradict and prevent his master's absurdities. Now it is the other way round. Sancho improvises a scene after the fashion of the romances of chivalry, while Don Quijote's ability to transform events to harmonize with his illusion breaks down before the crude vulgarity of the sight of the peasant woman. All this seems most significant. As we have here (intentionally) presented it, it sounds sad, bitter, and almost tragic.

But if we merely read Cervantes' text, we have a farce, and a farce which is overwhelmingly comic. Many illustrators have rendered the scene: Don Quijote on his knees beside Sancho, staring in wide-eyed bewilderment at the repellent spectacle before him. But only the stylistic contrast in the speeches, and the grotesque movement at the end (Dulcinea's fall and remounting), afford the fullest enjoyment of what is going on. The stylistic contrast in the speeches develops only slowly, because at first the peasant women are much too astonished. Dulcinea's first utterance (her request to be allowed to pass) is still moderate. It is only in their later speeches that the peasant women display the pearls of their eloquence. The first representative of the chivalric style is Sancho, and it is amusing and surprising to see how well he plays his part. He jumps off his donkey, throws himself at the women's feet, and speaks as though he had never heard anything in all his life but the jargon of romances of chivalry. Forms of address, syntax, metaphors, epithets, the description of his master's posture, and his supplication to be heard—it all comes out most successfully, although Sancho cannot read and owes his education wholly to the example set him by Don Quijote. His performance is successful, at least insofar as he gets his master to follow suit: Don Quijote kneels down beside him.

It might be supposed that all this would bring on a terrible crisis. Dulcinea is really *la señora de sus pensamientos*, the paragon of beauty, the goal and meaning of his life. Arousing his expectations in this way, and then disappointing them so greatly, is no harmless experiment. It could produce a shock which in turn could bring on much deeper insanity. But there is also the possibility that the shock might bring about a cure, instantaneous liberation from his idée fixe. Neither of these things happens. Don Quijote surmounts the shock. In his idée fixe itself he finds a solution which prevents him both from falling into despair and from recovering his sanity: Dulcinea is enchanted. This solution appears each time the exterior situation establishes itself as in insuperable contrast to the illusion. It makes it possible for Don Quijote to persist in the attitude of the noble and invincible hero persecuted by a powerful magician who envies his glory. In this particular case—the case of Dulcinea—the idea of so repellent and base an enchantment is certainly hard to endure. Still, it is possible to meet the situation by means available within the realm of the illusion itself, that is, by means of the knightly virtues of unalterable loyalty, devoted self-sacrifice, and unhesitating courage. And then there is the established fact that virtue will win in the end. The happy ending is a foregone conclusion. Thus both tragedy and cure are circumvented. And so, after a brief pause of disconcerted silence, Don Quijote begins to speak. He turns to Sancho first. His words show that he has recovered his bearings, that he has interpreted the situation in terms of his illusion. This interpretation has become so firmly crystallized in him that even the earthy colloquialisms in the directly preceding speech of one of the peasant women—however sharply they may contrast with the elevated style of knightly refinement—can no longer make him doubtful of his attitude. Sancho's stratagem has succeeded. Don Quijote's second sentence is addressed to Dulcinea.

It is a very beautiful sentence. A moment ago we pointed out how cleverly and amusingly Sancho handles the style of the romances of chivalry which he has picked up from his master. Now we see what sort of a master he had. The sentence begins, like a prayer, with an imploring apostrophe (*invocatio*). This has three gradations (*extremo del valor* . . . , *término* . . . , *único remedio* . . .), and they are very carefully considered and arranged, for it first emphasizes an absolute perfection, then a perfection in human terms, and finally the special personal devotion of the speaker. The threefold structure is held together by the initial words *y tú*, and ends, in its third, sweepingly constructed division, with the rhythmically conventional but magnificently integrated *corazón que te adora*. Here, in content, choice of words, and rhythm, the theme which appears at the end is already alluded to. Thus a transition is established from the *invocatio* to its obligatory complement, the *supplicatio*, for which the optative principal clause is reserved (*no dejes de mirarme* . . .), although it is still some time before we are allowed to reach it. First we have the multiple gradation—dramatically contrasting with both *invocatio* and *supplicatio*—of the concessive complex, *ya que* . . . , *y* . . . *y* . . . , *si ya también*. . . . Its sense is "and even though," and its rhythmic climax is reached in the middle of the first (*ya que*) part, in the strongly emphasized words *y para sólo ellos*. Only after this entire wonderful and dramatic melody of the concessive clause has run its course, is the long-restrained principal clause of the *supplicatio* allowed to appear, but it too holds back and piles up paraphrases and pleonasms until finally the main motif, which constitutes the goal and purpose of the entire period, is sounded: the words which are to symbolize Don Quijote's present attitude and his entire life, *la humildad con que mi alma te adora*. This is the style so greatly admired by Sancho in part 1, chapter 25, where Don Quijote reads his letter to Dulcinea aloud to him: *¡y como que le dice vuestra merced ahí todo cuanto quiere, y qué bien que encaja en la firma El Caballero de la Triste Figura!* But the present speech is incomparably more beautiful; with all its art it shows less pedantic preciosity than the letter. Cervantes is very fond of such rhythmically and pictorially rich, such beautifully articulated and musical bravura pieces of chivalric rhetoric (which are nevertheless rooted in the tradition of antiquity). And he is a master in the field. Here again he is not merely a destructive critic but a continuer and consummator of the great epico-rhetorical tradition for which prose too is an art. As soon as great emotions and passions or sublime events are involved, this elevated style with all its devices appears. To be sure, its being so long a convention has shifted it slightly from the sphere of high tragedy toward that of the smoothly pleasant, which is capable of at least a trace of self-irony. Yet it is still dominant in the serious sphere. One has only to read Dorotea's speech to her unfaithful lover (part 1, chapter 36), with its numerous figures, similes, and rhythmic clauses, in order to sense that this style is still alive even in the serious and the tragic.

Here, however, in Dulcinea's presence, it simply serves the effect of contrast. The peasant girl's crude, contemptuous reply gives it its real significance; we are in the realm of the low style, and Don Quijote's elevated rhetoric only serves to make the comedy of the stylistic anti-climax fully effective. But even this is not enough to satisfy Cervantes. To the stylistic anticlimax he adds an extreme anticlimax in the action by having Dulcinea fall off her donkey and jump on again with grotesque dexterity, while Don Quijote still tries to maintain the chivalric style. His being so firmly fixed in his illusion that neither Dulcinea's reply nor the scene with the donkey can shake him is the acme of farce. Even Sancho's exuberant gaiety (*Vive Roque*), which after all is nothing short of impertinent, cannot make him lose his bearings. He looks after the peasant women as they ride away, and when they have disappeared he turns to Sancho with words expressive much less of sadness or despair than of a sort of triumphant satisfaction over the fact that he has become the target of the evil magician's darkest arts. This makes it possible for him to feel that he is elect, unique, and in a way which tallies perfectly with the conventions of the knight-errant: *yo nací para ejemplo de desdichados, y para ser blanco y terrero donde tomen la mira y asesten las flechas de la mala fortuna*. And the observation he now makes, to the effect that the evil enchantment affects even Dulcinea's aura—for her breath had not been pleasant—can disturb his illusion as little as Sancho's grotesque description of details of her beauty. Encouraged by the complete success of his trick,

Sancho has now really warmed up and begins to play with his master's madness purely for his own amusement.

In our study we are looking for representations of everyday life in which that life is treated seriously, in terms of its human and social problems or even of its tragic complications. The scene from Don Quijote with which we are dealing is certainly realistic. All the participants are presented in their true reality, their living everyday existence. Not only the peasant women but Sancho too, not only Sancho but also Don Quijote, appear as persons representative of contemporary Spanish life. For the fact that Sancho is playing a rogue's game and that Don Quijote is enmeshed in his illusion does not raise either of them out of his everyday existence. Sancho is a peasant from La Mancha, and Don Quijote is no Amadis or Roland, but a little country squire who has lost his mind. At best we might say that the hidalgo's madness translates him into another, imaginary sphere of life; but even so the everyday character of our scene and others similar to it remains unharmed, because the persons and events of everyday life are constantly colliding with his madness and come out in stronger relief through the contrast.

It is much more difficult to determine the position of the scene, and of the novel as a whole, on the scale of levels between tragic and comic. As presented, the story of the encounter with the three peasant women is nothing if not comic. The idea of having Don Quijote encounter a concrete Dulcinea must certainly have come to Cervantes even when he was writing the first part of the novel. The idea of building up such a scene on the basis of a deceitful trick played by Sancho, so that the roles appear interchanged, is a stroke of genius, and it is so magnificently carried out that the farce presents itself to the reader as something perfectly natural and even bound to take place, despite the complex absurdity of all its presuppositions and relations. But it remains pure farce. We have tried to show above that, in the case of the only one of the participants with whom the possibility of a shift into the tragic and problematic exists, that is, the case of Don Quijote, such a shift is definitely avoided. The fact that he almost instantaneously and as it were automatically takes refuge in the interpretation that Dulcinea is under an enchantment excludes everything tragic. He is taken in, and this time even by Sancho; he kneels down and orates in a lofty emotional style before a group of ugly peasant women; and then he takes pride in his sublime misfortune.

But Don Quijote's feelings are genuine and profound. Dulcinea is really the mistress of his thoughts; he is truly filled with the spirit of a mission which he regards as man's highest duty. He is really true, brave, and ready to sacrifice everything. So unconditional a feeling and so unconditional a determination impose admiration even though they are based on a foolish illusion, and this admiration has been accorded to Don Quijote by almost all readers. There are probably few lovers of literature who do not associate the concept of ideal greatness with Don Quijote. It may be absurd, fantastic, grotesque; but it is still ideal, unconditional, heroic. It is especially since the Romantic period that this conception has become almost universal, and it withstands all attempts on the part of philological criticism to show that Cervantes' intention was not to produce such an impression.

The difficulty lies in the fact that in Don Quijote's idée fixe we have a combination of the noble, immaculate, and redeeming with absolute nonsense. A tragic struggle for the ideal and desirable cannot at first blush be imagined in any way but as intervening meaningfully in the actual state of things, stirring it up, pressing it hard; with the result that the meaningful ideal encounters an equally meaningful resistance which proceeds either from inertia, petty malice, and envy, or possibly from a more conservative view. The will working for an ideal must accord with existing reality at least to such an extent that it meets it, so that the two interlock and a real conflict arises. Don Quijote's idealism is not of this kind. It is not based on an understanding of actual conditions in this world. Don Quijote does have such an understanding but it deserts him as soon as the idealism of his idée fixe takes hold of him. Everything he does in that state is completely senseless and so incompatible with the existing world that it produces only comic confusion there. It not only has no chance of success, it actually has no point of contact with reality; it expends itself in a vacuum.

The same idea can be developed in another way, so that further consequences become clear. The theme of the noble and brave fool who sets forth to realize his ideal and improve the world, might be treated in such a way that the problems and conflicts in the world are presented and worked out in the process. Indeed, the purity and ingenuousness of the fool could be such that, even in the absence of any concrete purpose to produce effects, wherever he appears he unwittingly goes to the heart of things, so that the conflicts which are pending and hidden are rendered acute. One might think here of Dostoevski's *Idiot*. Thus the fool could be involved in responsibility and guilt and assume the role of a tragic figure. Nothing of the sort takes place in Cervantes' novel.

Don Quijote's encounter with Dulcinea is not a good illustration of his relationship to concrete reality, inasmuch as here he does not, as elsewhere, impose his ideal will in conflict with that reality; here he beholds and worships the incarnation of his ideal. Yet this encounter too is symbolic of the mad knight's relationship to the phenomena of this world. The reader should recall what traditional concepts were contained in the Dulcinea motif and how they are echoed in Sancho's and Don Quijote's grotesquely sublime words. *La señora de sus pensamientos, extremo del valor que puede desearse, término de la humana gentileza*, and so forth—alive in all this are Plato's idea of beauty, courtly love, the *donna gentile* of the *dolce stil nuovo*, Beatrice, *la gloriosa donna della mia mente*. And all this ammunition is expended on three ugly and vulgar peasant women. It is poured into a void. Don Quijote can neither be graciously received nor graciously rejected. There is nothing but amusingly senseless confusion. To find anything serious, or a concealed deeper meaning in this scene, one must violently overinterpret it.

The three women are flabbergasted; they get away as fast as they can. This is an effect frequently produced by Don Quijote's appearance. Often disputes result and the participants come to blows. People are apt to lose their temper when Don Quijote interferes in their business with his nonsense. Very often too they humor him in his idée fixe in order to get some fun from it. The innkeeper and the whores at the time of his first departure react in this way. The same thing happens again later with the company at the second inn, with the priest and the barber, Dorotea and Don Fernando, and even with Maritornes. Some of these, it is true, mean to use their game as a way of getting the knight safely back home, but they carry it much further than their practical purpose would require. In part 2 the *bachiller* Sansón Carrasco bases his therapeutic plan on playing along with Don Quijote's idée fixe; later, at the duke's palace and in Barcelona, his madness is methodically exploited as a pastime, so that hardly any of his adventures are genuine; they are simply staged, that is, they have been especially prepared to suit the hidalgo's madness, for the amusement of those who get them up. Among all these reactions, both in part 1 and part 2, one thing is completely lacking: tragic complications and serious consequences. Even the element of contemporary satire and criticism is very weak. If we leave out of consideration the purely literary criticism, there is almost none at all. It is limited to brief remarks or occasional caricatures of types (for example the priest at the duke's court). It never goes to the roots of things and is moderate in attitude. Above all, Don Quijote's adventures never reveal any of the basic problems of the society of the time. His activity reveals nothing at all. It affords an opportunity to present Spanish life in its color and fullness. In the resulting clashes between Don Quijote and reality no situation ever results which puts in question that reality's right to be what it is. It is always right and he wrong; and after a bit of amusing confusion it flows calmly on, untouched. There is one scene where this might seem doubtful. It is the freeing of the galley slaves in part 1, chapter 22. Here Don Quijote intervenes in the established legal order, and some critics will be found to uphold the opinion that he does so in the name of a higher morality. This view is natural, for what Don Quijote says: *allá se lo haya cada uno con su pecado;*

*Dios hay en el cielo que no se descuida de castigar al malo ni de premiar al bueno, y
no es bien que los hombres honrados sean verdugos do los otros hombres, no yéndoles
nada en ello*—such a statement is certainly on a higher level than any positive
law. But a "higher morality" of the kind here envisaged must be consistent
and methodical if it is to be taken seriously. We know, however, that Don
Quijote has no idea of making a basic attack on the established legal order.
He is neither an anarchist nor a prophet of the Kingdom of God. On the
contrary, it is apparent again and again that whenever his idée fixe happens
not to be involved he is willing to conform, that it is only through his idée
fixe that he claims a special position for the knight-errant. The beautiful
words, *alla se lo haya*, etc., are deeply rooted, to be sure, in the kindly wisdom
of his real nature (this is a point to which we shall return), but in their context
they are still merely an improvisation. It is his idée fixe which determines him
to free the prisoners. It alone forces him to conceive of everything he
encounters as the subject of a knightly adventure. It supplies him with the
motifs "help the distressed" or "free the victims of force," and he acts
accordingly. I think it wholly erroneous to look for a matter of principle here,
for anything like a conflict between natural Christian and positive law. For
such a conflict, moreover, an opponent would have to appear, someone like
the Grand Inquisitor in Dostoevski, who would be authorized and willing to
represent the cause of positive law against Don Quijote. His Majesty's
commissary who is in charge of the convoy of prisoners is neither suited for
the role nor prepared to play it. Personally he may very well be ready to
accept the argument, "judge not that ye be not judged." But he has passed no
judgment; he is no representative of positive law. He has his instructions and
is quite justified in appealing to them.

Everything comes out all right, and time and again the damage done
or suffered by Don Quijote is treated with stoic humor as a matter of comic
confusion. Even the *bachiller* Alonso Lopez, as he lies on the ground, badly
mauled and with one leg pinned under his mule, consoles himself with
mocking puns. This scene occurs in chapter 19 of book 1. It also shows that
Don Quijote's idée fixe saves him from feeling responsible for the harm he
does, so that in his conscience too every form of tragic conflict and somber
seriousness is obviated. He has acted in accordance with the rules of
knight-errantry, and so he is justified. To be sure, he hastens to assist the
bachiller, for he is a kind and helpful soul; but it does not occur to him to
feel guilty. Nor does he feel any guiltier when at the beginning of chapter
30 the priest puts him to the test by telling what evil effects his freeing of
the prisoners had produced. He angrily exclaims that it is the duty of a
knight-errant to help those in distress but not to judge whether their plight
is deserved or not. And that settles the question as far as he is concerned.

In part 2, where the gaiety is even more relaxed and elegant, such complications no longer occur at all.

There is, then, very little of problem and tragedy in Cervantes' book—and yet it belongs among the literary masterpieces of an epoch during which the modern problematic and tragic conception of things arose in the European mind. Don Quijote's madness reveals nothing of the sort. The whole book is a comedy in which well-founded reality holds madness up to ridicule.

And yet Don Quijote is not only ridiculous. He is not like the bragging soldier or the comic old man or the pedantic and ignorant doctor. In our scene Don Quijote is taken in by Sancho. But does Sancho despise him and deceive him all the way through? Not at all. He deceives him only because he sees no other way out. He loves and reveres him, although he is half conscious (and sometimes fully conscious) of his madness. He learns from him and refuses to part with him. In Don Quijote's company he becomes cleverer and better than he was before. With all his madness, Don Quijote preserves a natural dignity and superiority which his many miserable failures cannot harm. He is not vulgar, as the above-mentioned comic types normally are. Actually he is not a "type" at all in this sense, for on the whole he is no automaton producing comic effects. He even develops, and grows kinder and wiser while his madness persists. But would it be true to say that his is a wise madness in the ironical sense of the romanticists? Does wisdom come to him through his madness? Does his madness give him an understanding he could not have attained in soundness of mind, and do we hear wisdom speak through madness in his case as we do with Shakespeare's fools or with Charlie Chaplin? No, that is not it either. As soon as his madness, that is, that idée fixe of knight-errantry, takes hold of him, he acts unwisely, he acts like an automaton in the manner of the comic types mentioned above. He is wise and kind independently of his madness. A madness like this, it is true, can arise only in a pure and noble soul, and it is also true that wisdom, kindness, and decency shine through his madness and make it appear lovable. Yet his wisdom and his madness are clearly separated—in direct contrast to what we find in Shakespeare, the fools of Romanticism, and Charlie Chaplin. The priest says it as early as chapter 30 of part 1, and later it comes out again and again: he is mad only when his idée fixe comes into play; otherwise he is a perfectly normal and very intelligent individual. His madness is not such that it represents his whole nature and is completely identical with it. At a specific moment an idée fixe laid hold on him; but even so it leaves parts of his being unaffected, so that in many instances he acts and speaks like a person of sound mind; and one day, shortly before his death, it leaves him again. He was some fifty years of age when, under the influence of his excessive reading of romances of chivalry, he conceived his absurd plan. This is strange. An overwrought state of mind resulting from solitary reading might rather be expected in a youthful person (Julien Sorel, Madame Bovary), and one is tempted to look for a specific psychological explanation. How is it possible that a man in his fifties who leads a normal life and whose intelligence is well-developed in many ways and not at all unbalanced, should embark upon so absurd a venture? In the opening sentences of his novel Cervantes supplies some details of his hero's social position. From them we may at best infer that it was burdensome to him, for it offered no possibility of an active life commensurate with his abilities. He was as it were paralyzed by the limitations imposed upon him on the one hand by his class and on the other by his poverty. Thus one might suppose that his mad decision represents a flight from a situation which has become unbearable, a violent attempt to emancipate himself from it. This sociological and psychological interpretation has been advocated by various writers on the subject. I myself advanced it in an earlier passage of this book, and I leave it there because in the context of that passage it is justified. But as an interpretation of Cervantes' artistic purpose it is unsatisfactory, for it is not likely that he intended his brief observations on Don Quijote's social position and habits of life to imply anything like a psychological motivation of the knight's idée fixe. He would have had to state it more clearly and elaborate it in greater detail. A modern psychologist might find still other explanations of Don Quijote's strange madness. But this sort of approach to the problem has no place in Cervantes' thinking. Confronted with the question of the causes of Don Quijote's madness, he has only one answer: Don Quijote read too many romances of chivalry and they deranged his mind. That this should happen to a man in his fifties can be explained—from within the work—only in aesthetic terms, that is, through the comic vision which came to Cervantes when he conceived the novel: a tall, elderly man, dressed in old-fashioned and shabby armor, a picture which is beautifully expressive not only of madness but also of asceticism and the fanatic pursuit of an ideal. We simply have to accept the fact that this cultured and intelligent country gentleman goes suddenly mad—not, like Ajax or Hamlet, because of a terrible shock—but simply because he has read too many romances of chivalry. Here again there is nothing tragic. In the analysis of his madness we have to do without the concept of the tragic, just as we have to do without the specifically Shakespearean and romantic combination of wisdom and madness in which one cannot be conceived without the other.

Don Quijote's wisdom is not the wisdom of a fool. It is the intelligence, the nobility, the civility, and the dignity of a gifted and well-balanced man— a man neither demonic nor paradoxical, not beset by doubt and indecision nor by any feeling of not being at home in this world, but even-tempered, able to weigh and ponder, receptive, and lovable and modest even in his irony. Furthermore he is a conservative, or at least essentially in accord with the order of things as it is. This comes out wherever and whenever he deals with people—especially with Sancho Panza—in the longer or shorter intervals during which his idée fixe is quiescent. From the very beginning—although more in part 2 than in part 1—the kindly, intelligent, and amiable figure, Alsonso Quijano el bueno, whose most distinguishing characteristic is his naturally superior dignity, coexists with the mad adventurer. We need only read with what kindly and merry irony he treats Sancho in part 2 chapter 7, when the latter, on the advice of his wife Teresa, begins to present his request for a fixed salary. His madness intervenes only when he justifies his refusal by referring to the customs of knights-errant. Passages of this kind abound. There is evidence everywhere that we have to do with an intelligent Don Quijote and a mad one, side by side, and that his intelligence is in no way dialectically inspired by his madness but is a normal and, as it were, average intelligence.

That in itself yields an unusual combination. There are levels of tone represented here which one is not accustomed to finding in purely comic contexts. A fool is a fool. We are used to seeing him represented on a single plane, that of the comic and foolish, with which, at least in earlier literature, baseness and stupidity, and at times underhanded malice, were connected as well. But what are we to say of a fool who is at the same time wise, with that wisdom which seems the least compatible with folly, that is, the wisdom of intelligent moderation? This very fact, this combination of intelligent moderation with absurd excess results in a multiplicity which cannot be made to accord altogether with the purely comic. But that is by no means all. It is on the very wings of his madness that his wisdom soars upward, that it roams the world and becomes richer there. For if Don Quijote had not gone mad, he would not have left his house. And then Sancho too would have stayed home, and he could never have drawn from his innate being the things which—as we find in delighted amazement—were potentially contained in it. The multifarious play of action and reaction between the two and their joint play in the world would not have taken place.

This play, as we think we have been able to show, is never tragic; and never are human problems, whether personal or social, represented in such a way that we tremble and are moved to compassion. We always remain in the realm of gaiety. But the levels of gaiety are multiplied as never before. Let us return once more to the text from which we set out. Don Quijote speaks to the peasant women in a style which is genuinely the elevated style of courtly love and which in itself is by no means grotesque. His sentences are not at all ridiculous (though they may seem so to many readers in our day), they are in the tradition of the period and represent a masterpiece of elevated expression in the form in which it was then alive. If it was Cervantes' purpose to attack the romances of chivalry (and there can be no doubt that it was), he nevertheless did not attack the elevated style of chivalric expression. On the contrary, he reproaches the romances of chivalry with not mastering the style, with being stylistically wooden and dry. And so it comes about that in the middle of a parody against the knightly ideology of love we find one of the most beautiful prose passages which the late form of the tradition of courtly love produced. The peasant women answer with characteristic coarseness. Such a rustically boorish style had long been employed in comic literature (although possibly never with the same balance between moderation and verve), but what had certainly never happened before was that it should follow directly upon a speech like Don Quijote's—a speech which, taken by itself, could never make us suspect that it occurs in a grotesque context. The motif of a knight begging a peasant woman to hear his love—a motif which produces a comparable situation—is age old. It is the motif of the *pastourelle*; it was in favor with the early Provençal poets, and, as we shall see when we come to Voltaire, it was remarkably long-lived. However, in the *pastourelle* the two partners have adapted themselves to each other; they understand each other; and the result is a homogeneous level of style on the borderline between the idyllic and the everyday. In Cervantes' case, the two realms of life and style clash by reason of Don Quijote's madness. There is no possibility of a transition; each is closed in itself; and the only link that holds them together is the merry neutrality of the playful scheme of puppet-master Sancho—the awkward bumpkin, who but a short time before believed almost everything his master said, who will never get over believing some of it, and who always acts in accordance with the momentary situation. In our passage the dilemma of the moment has inspired him to deceive his master; and he adapts himself to the position of puppet-master with as much gusto and elasticity as he later will to the position of governor of an island. He starts the play in the elevated style, then switches to the low—not, however, in the manner of the peasant woman. He maintains his superiority and remains master of the situation which he has himself created under the pressure of necessity but which he now enjoys to the full.

What Sancho does in this case—assuming a role, transforming himself, and playing with his master's madness—other characters in the book are perpetually doing. Don Quijote's madness gives rise to an inexhaustible series of disguises and histrionics: Dorotea in the role of Princess Micomicona, the barber as her page, Sansón Carrasco as knight-errant,

Ginés de Pasamonte as puppet-master—these are but a few examples. Such
metamorphoses make reality become a perpetual stage without ever ceasing
to be reality. And when the characters do not submit to the metamorphosis
of their own free will, Don Quijote's madness forces them into their roles—
as happens time and again, beginning with the innkeeper and the whores in
the first tavern. Reality willingly cooperates with a play which dresses it up
differently every moment. It never spoils the gaiety of the play by bringing
in the serious weight of its troubles, cares, and passions. All that is resolved
in Don Quijote's madness; it transforms the real everyday world into a gay
stage. Here one should recall the various adventures with women which
occur in the course of the narrative in addition to the encounter with
Dulcinea: Maritornes struggling in Don Quijote's arms, Dorotea as Princess
Micomicona, the lovelorn Altisidora's serenade, the nocturnal encounter
with Doña Rodriguez (a scene which Cide Hamete Benengeli says that he
would have given his best coat to see)—each of these stories is in a different
style; each contains a shift in stylistic level; all of them are resolved by Don
Quijote's madness, and all of them remain within the realm of gaiety. And yet
there are several which need not necessarily have been thus restricted. The
description of Maritornes and her muleteer is coarsely realistic; Dorotea is
unhappy; and Doña Rodriguez is in great distress of mind because her
daughter has been seduced. Don Quijote's intervention changes nothing of
this—neither Maritornes' loose life nor the sad plight of Doña Rodriguez'
daughter. But what happens is that we are not concerned over these things,
that we see the lot and the life of these women through the prism of gaiety,
and that our consciences do not feel troubled over them. As God lets the sun
shine and the rain fall on the just and the unjust alike, so Don Quijote's
madness, in its bright equanimity, illumines everything that crosses his path
and leaves it in a state of gay confusion.

The most varied suspense and wisest gaiety of the book are revealed in
a relationship which Don Quijote maintains throughout: his relationship
with Sancho Panza. It is not at all as easy to describe in unambiguous terms
as the relationship between Rocinante and Sancho's donkey or that between
the donkey and Sancho himself. They are not always united in unfailing
loyalty and love. It frequently happens that Don Quijote becomes so angry
with Sancho that he abuses and maltreats him; at times he is ashamed of him;
and once—in part 2, chapter 27—he actually deserts him in danger. Sancho,
for his part, originally accompanies Don Quijote because he is stupid and for
the selfishly materialistic reason that he expects fantastic advantages from the
venture, and also because, despite all its hardships, he prefers a vagabond life
to the regular working hours and monotony of life at home. Before long he
begins to sense that something must be wrong with Don Quijote's mind, and

then he sometimes deceives him, makes fun of him, and speaks of him disrespectfully. At times, even in part 2, he is so disgusted and disillusioned that he is all but ready to leave Don Quijote. Again and again the reader is made to see how variable and composite our human relationships are, how capricious and dependent on the moment even the most intimate of them. In the passage which was our point of departure Sancho deceives his master and plays almost cruelly on his madness. But what painstaking humoring of Don Quijote's madness, what sympathetic penetration of his world, must have preceded Sancho's conceiving such a plan and his being able to act his role so well! Only a few months earlier he had not the slightest inkling of all this. Now he lives, after his own fashion, in the world of knightly adventure; he is fascinated by it. He has fallen in love with his master's madness and with his own role. His development is most amazing. Yet withal, he is and remains Sancho, of the Panza family, a Christian of the old stock, well known in his village. He remains all that even in the role of a wise governor and also—and indeed especially—when he insists on Sanchica's marrying nothing less than a count. He remains Sancho; and all that happens to him could happen only to Sancho. But the fact that these things do happen, that his body and his mind are put in such violent commotion and emerge from the ordeal in all their unshakable and idiosyncratic genuineness—this he owes to Don Quijote, *su amo y natural señor*. The experience of Don Quijote's personality is not received by anyone as completely as it is by Sancho; it is not assimilated pure and whole by anyone as it is by him. The others all wonder about him, are amused or angered by him, or try to cure him. Sancho lives himself into Don Quijote, whose madness and wisdom become productive in him. Although he has far too little critical reasoning power to form and express a synthetic judgment upon him, it is still he, in all his reactions, through whom we best understand Don Quijote. And this in turn binds Don Quijote to him. Sancho is his consolation and his direct opposite, his creature and yet an independent fellow being who holds out against him and prevents his madness from locking him up as though in solitary confinement. Two partners who appear together as contrasting comic or semi-comic figures represent a very old motif which has retained its effectiveness even today in farce, caricature, the circus, and the film: the tall thin man and the short fat one; the clever man and his stupid companion; master and servant; the refined aristocrat and the simple-minded peasants; and whatever other combinations and variants there may be in different countries and under different cultural conditions. What Cervantes made of it is magnificent and unique.

Perhaps it is not quite correct to speak of what Cervantes made of it. It may be more exact to say "what became of the motif in his hands." For centuries—and especially since the romanticists—many things have been read into him which he hardly foreboded, let alone intended. Such transforming and transcendent interpretations are often fertile. A book like *Don Quijote* dissociates itself from its author's intention and leads a life of its own. Don Quijote shows a new face to every age which enjoys him. Yet the historian—whose task it is to define the place of a given work in a historical continuity—must endeavor insofar as that is still possible, to attain a clear understanding of what the work meant to its author and his contemporaries. I have tried to interpret as little as possible. In particular, I have pointed out time and again how little there is in the text which can be called tragic and problematic. I take it as merry play on many levels, including in particular the level of everyday realism. The latter differentiates it from the equally unproblematic gaiety of let us say Ariosto; but even so it remains play. This means that no matter how painstakingly I have tried to do as little interpreting as possible, I yet cannot help feeling that my thoughts about the book often go far beyond Cervantes' aesthetic intention. Whatever that intention may have been (we shall not here take up the problems presented by the aesthetics of his time), it most certainly did not consciously and from the beginning propose to create a relationship like that between Don Quijote and Sancho Panza as we see it after having read the novel. Rather, the two figures were first a single vision, and what finally developed from them—singly and together—arose gradually, as the result of hundreds of individual ideas, as the result of hundreds of situations in which Cervantes puts them and to which they react on the spur of the moment, as the result of the inexhaustible, ever fresh power of the poetic imagination. Now and again there are actual incongruities and contradictions, not only in matters of fact (which has often been noted) but also in psychology: developments which do not fit into the total picture of the two heroes—which indicates how much Cervantes allowed himself to be guided by the momentary situation, by the demands of the adventure in hand. This is still the case—more frequently even—in part 2. Gradually and without any preconceived plan, the two personages evolve, each in himself and also in their relation to each other. To be sure, this is the very thing which allows what is peculiarly Cervantean, the sum of Cervantes' experience of life and the wealth of his imagination, to enter the episodes and speeches all the more richly and spontaneously. The "peculiarly Cervantean" can not be described in words. And yet I shall attempt to say something *about* it in order to clarify its power and its limits. First of all it is something spontaneously sensory: a vigorous capacity for the vivid visualization of very different people in very varied situations, for the vivid realization and expression of what thoughts enter their minds, what emotions fill their hearts, and what words come to their lips. This capacity he possesses so directly and strongly, and in a manner so independent of any sort of ulterior motive, that almost everything realistic written before him appears limited, conventional, or propagandistic in comparison. And just as sensory is his capacity to think up or hit upon ever new combinations of people and events. Here, to be sure, we have to consider the older tradition of the romance of adventure and its renewal through Boiardo and Ariosto, but no one before him had infused the element of genuine everyday reality into that brilliant and purposeless play of combinations. And finally he has a "something" which organizes the whole and makes it appear in a definite "Cervantean" light. Here things begin to be very difficult. One might avoid the difficulty and say that this "something" is merely contained in the subject matter, in the idea of the country gentleman who loses his mind and convinces himself that it is his duty to revive knight-errantry, that it is this theme which gives the book its unity and its attitude. But the theme (which Cervantes, by the way, took over from the minor and in itself totally uninteresting contemporary work, the *Entremés de los romances*) could have been treated quite differently too. The hero might have looked very different; it was not necessary that there should be a Dulcinea and particularly a Sancho. But above all, what was it that so attracted Cervantes in the idea? What attracted him was the possibilities it offered for multifariousness and effects of perspective, the mixture of fanciful and everyday elements in the subject, its malleability, elasticity, adaptability. It was ready to absorb all forms of style and art. It permitted the presentation of the most variegated picture of the world in a light congenial to his own nature. And here we have come back to the difficult question we asked before: what is the "something" which orders the whole and makes it appear in a definite, "Cervantean" light?

It is not a philosophy; it is no didactic purpose; it is not even a being stirred by the uncertainty of human existence or by the power of destiny, as in the case of Montaigne and Shakespeare. It is an attitude—an attitude toward the world, and hence also toward the subject matter of his art—in which bravery and equanimity play a major part. Together with the delight he takes in the multifariousness of his sensory play there is in him a certain Southern reticence and pride. This prevents him from taking the play very seriously. He looks at it; he shapes it; he finds it diverting; it is also intended to afford the reader refined intellectual diversion.

But he does not take sides (except against badly written books); he remains neutral. It is not enough to say that he does not judge and draws no conclusions: the case is not even called, the questions are not even asked. No one and nothing (except bad books and plays) is condemned in the book: neither Ginés de Pasamonte nor Roque Guinart, neither Maritornes nor Zoraida. For us Zoraida's behavior toward her father becomes a moral problem which we cannot help pondering; but Cervantes tells the story without giving a hint of his thoughts on the subject. Or rather, it is not Cervantes himself who tells the story, but the prisoner—who naturally finds Zoraida's behavior commendable. And that settles the matter. There are a few caricatures in the book—the Biscayan, the priest at the duke's castle, Doña Rodriguez; but these raise no ethical problems and imply no basic judgments.

On the other hand no one is praised as exemplary either. Here one might think of the Knight of the Green Caftan, Don Diego de Miranda, who in part 2, chapter 16, gives a description of his temperate style of life and thereby makes such a profound impression upon Sancho. He is temperate and inclined to rational deliberation; in dealing with both Don Quijote and Sancho he finds the right tone of benevolent, modest, and yet self-assured politeness. His attempts to confute or mitigate Don Quijote's madness are friendly and understanding. He must not be put with the narrow-minded and intolerant priest at the duke's court (as has been done by the distinguished Spanish scholar, Américo Castro). Don Diego is a paragon of his class, the Spanish variety of the humanist nobleman: *otium cum dignitate*. But he certainly is no more than that. He is no absolute model. For that, after all, he is too cautious and too mediocre, and it is quite possible (so far Castro may be right) that there is a shade of irony in the manner in which Cervantes describes his style of life, his manner of hunting, and his views on his son's literary inclinations.

Cervantes' attitude is such that his world becomes play in which every participating figure is justified by the simple fact of living in a given place. Only Don Quijote in his madness is not justified, is wrong. He is also wrong, absolutely speaking, as against the temperate and peaceable Don Diego, whom Cervantes—"with inspired perversity," as Castro puts it—makes the witness of the adventure with the lion. It would be forcing things if one sought to see here a glorification of adventurous heroism as against calculating, petty, and mediocre caution. If there is possibly an undertone of irony in the portrait of Don Diego, Don Quijote is not possibly but unqualifiedly conceived not with an undertone of ridicule but as ridiculous through and through. The chapter is introduced by a description of the absurd pride he takes in his victory over Carrasco (disguised as a knight) and a conversation on this theme with Sancho. The passage bears rereading for the sake of the realization it affords that there is hardly another instance in the entire book where Don Quijote is ridiculed—also in ethical terms—as he is here. The description of himself with which he introduces himself to Don Diego is foolish and turgid. It is in this state of mind that he takes on the adventure with the lion. And the lion does nothing but turn its back on Don

Quijote! This is pure parody. And the additional details are fit for parody too: Don Quijote's request that the guard should give him a written testimonial to his heroism; the way he receives Sancho; his decision to change his name (henceforth he will be the Knight of the Lion), and many others.

Don Quijote alone is wrong as long as he is mad. He alone is wrong in a well-ordered world in which everybody else has his right place. He himself comes to see this in the end when, dying, he finds his way back into the order of the world. But is it true that the world is well-ordered? The question is not raised. Certain it is that in the light of Don Quijote's madness and confronted with it, the world appears well-ordered and even as merry play. There may be a great deal of wretchedness, injustice, and disorder in it. We meet harlots, criminals as galley slaves, seduced girls, hanged bandits, and much more of the same sort. But all that does not perturb us. Don Quijote's appearance, which corrects nothing and helps no one, changes good and bad fortune into play.

The theme of the mad country gentleman who undertakes to revive knight-errantry gave Cervantes an opportunity to present the world as play in that spirit of multiple, perspective, non-judging, and even non-questioning neutrality which is a brave form of wisdom. It could very simply be expressed in the words of Don Quijote which have already been quoted: *allá se lo haya cada uno con su pecado, Dios hay en el cielo que no se descuida de castigar al malo, ni de premiar al bueno.* Or else in the words which he addresses to Sancho in part 2, chapter 8, at the end of the conversation about monks and knights: *muchos son los caminos por donde lleva Dios a los suyos al cielo.* This is as much as to say that in the last analysis it is a devout wisdom. It is not unrelated to the neutral attitude which Gustave Flaubert strove so hard to attain, and yet it is very different from it: Flaubert wanted to transform reality through style; transform it so that it would appear as God sees it, so that the divine order—insofar as it concerns the fragment of reality treated in a particular work—would perforce be incarnated in the author's style. For Cervantes, a good novel serves no other purpose than to afford refined recreation, *honesto entretenimiento.* No one has expressed this more convincingly in recent times than W. J. Entwistle in his book on Cervantes (1940) where he speaks of recreation and connects it very beautifully with re-creation. It would never have occurred to Cervantes that the style of a novel—be it the best of novels—could reveal the order of the universe. On the other hand, for him too the phenomena of reality had come to be difficult to survey and no longer possible to arrange in an unambiguous and traditional manner. Elsewhere in Europe men had long since begun to question and to doubt, and even to begin building anew with their own materials. But that was in keeping neither with the spirit of his country nor with his own temperament, nor finally with his conception of the office of a writer. He found the order of reality in play. It is no longer the play of Everyman, which provides fixed norms for the judgment of good and evil. That was still so in *La Celestina*. Now things are no longer so simple. Cervantes undertakes to pass judgment only in matters concerning his profession as a writer. So far as the secular world is concerned, we are all sinners; God will see to it that evil is punished and good rewarded. Here on earth the order of the unsurveyable is to be found in play. However arduous it may be to survey and judge phenomena, before the mad knight of La Mancha they turn into a dance of gay and diverting confusion.

This, it seems to me, is the function of Don Quijote's madness. When the theme—the mad hidalgo who sets forth to realize the ideal of the *caballero andante*—began to kindle Cervantes' imagination, he also perceived a vision of how, confronted with such madness, contemporary reality might be portrayed. And the vision pleased him, both by reason of its multifariousness and by reason of the neutral gaiety which the knight's madness spreads over everything which comes in contact with it. That it is a heroic and idealized form of madness, that it leaves room for wisdom and humanity, was no doubt equally pleasing to him. But to conceive of Don Quijote's madness in symbolic and tragic terms seems to me forced. That can be read into the text; it is not there of itself. So universal and multilayered, so noncritical and nonproblematic a gaiety in the portrayal of everyday reality has not been attempted again in European letters. I cannot imagine where and when it might have been attempted.

W. H. AUDEN

The Ironic Hero: Some Reflections on Don Quixote

The following remarks have to assume that the reaction of other readers to *Don Quixote* is the same as mine, namely, that it is a portrait of the Christian Saint. Granted this, it may be interesting to consider:

1. What are the artistic difficulties involved in attempting such a portrait?
2. How does Cervantes solve them?

The Hero

To be the hero or heroine of a book a person must be:

1. Interesting, i.e., either his character or the situation in which he finds himself must be exceptional, even unique.
2. Completely public, i.e., his character, his motives, his actions must become completely manifest to the reader even if they remain hidden from the hero himself, deducible even if not directly stated. This means that anything which happens or might happen to the hero which is not described is of no account.

From *Horizon* 20. © 1949 by *Horizon*.

Heroes are conventionally divided into three classes, the epic hero, the tragic hero, and the comic hero. Don Quixote fits none of them.

The Epic Hero

The epic hero is born with the gift of exceptional *areté*. By birth and breeding he is exceptionally strong, brave, handsome, etc. This *areté* is manifested in exceptional deeds, i.e., he performs feats of which the average is incapable. His motive is to win admiration from his equals whether they be friends or foes. The moral standard by which he lives is not a universal requirement, the law, but an individual one, honour. He is not tragic, i.e., he does not suffer more than others; but his death has exceptional pathos—the great warrior comes to the same end as the lowest churl. He exists in the present moment when he comes into collision with another heroic individual.

The Tragic Hero

All tragic heroes must (*a*) have some demonstrated *areté* in the epic sense, (*b*) move from glory to misery; their tragic character is manifested by their suffering more than the average. (*c*) This suffering is caused by a collision with the universal law of justice, which is the same for all. With this in common, there are, however, important differences between the classical and the Christian conceptions of the tragic hero, e.g.:

1. The former is placed in a situation where he is bound to become guilty of manifest sins. The sin for which he is responsible is the subjective sin of hybris. He is made to commit the others as a punishment. The situation of the latter is created partly by others, partly by himself. He is as responsible for the manifest sins he commits as he is for the invisible sin of pride which produces them. Further, there is a difference between hybris and pride. Hybris means believing that you *are* a god, i.e., that you cannot suffer; pride means a defiant attempt to *become* a god, when you secretly know that you are a mortal creature. The classical tragic hero is blind; the Christian tragic hero deceives himself.
2. The former, therefore, must be a fortunate and happy man. The latter (e.g. Richard III) need not be; he must only have an exceptionally strong defiant will.

3. The effect of suffering on the former is to make him humble;
    through suffering he expiates the past. The effect of suffering
    on the latter is to harden his heart for, if he repents, then he
    ceases to be tragic: e.g. Angelo in *Measure for Measure* and
    Lear are not tragic heroes. Othello is. The Christian tragic
    hero is damned.

The Comic Hero

In the comedy of situation (e.g. identical twins) the hero is not properly
so called, for he is the average man placed in a less dignified situation than
the average. The truly comic hero has less *areté* than the average, e.g., the
jealous old husband or the unsuccessful rogue. His attempt to violate the law
is thwarted not by the law but by other rogues who are equally outside the
law. Like the tragic hero he suffers; but (*a*) the spectator does not suffer
sympathetically because he does not identify himself with the comic hero
through admiration, (*b*) the suffering is temporary, (*c*) the suffering is
educational, i.e., it cures him of his comic madness so that he conforms with
the law, either through repentance or out of prudence.

The Christian Saint

The Christian Saint has no special *areté* of power or knowledge (such
as he may have is irrelevant), only an obedient will. He is virtuous out of faith
in and love of God and his neighbour, not out of a pride which wants him to
think well of himself.

To manifest this aesthetically is very difficult because:

a) He must be shown as failing in a worldly sense, i.e., as
    coming into collision with the law of this world, otherwise
    there is no proof that he acts out of faith and not mere
    worldly prudence.
b) Failure and suffering, however, are in themselves no proof of
    faith, because the collision with the law may also be the result
    of pride. The visible ends of Christ, the repentant thief and
    the unrepentant thief are the same, though the third is a
    tragic figure, the second one a comic figure in the
    profoundest sense, and Christ is not a hero at all, for he is not
    the Man-God (Hercules) but the God-Man.

c) The virtues produced by pride cannot be distinguished objectively from the virtues produced by faith. When Becket in *Murder in the Cathedral* is assailed by the fourth tempter, who suggests that he be martyred for self-glorification, it is impossible for Eliot to prove to us that Becket resists the temptation; he can only state that it exists.

d) It is possible, up to a point, to manifest hybris; Agamemnon walks on the purple carpet, Darius attempts to bridge the Hellespont, etc. Pride cannot be directly manifested, for it cannot be directly known even by its victims. I can look in the mirror of my conscience and learn that I am greedy, envious, lustful, etc., and from that infer that I am proud. I cannot, however, learn that I am proud because the pride, if it is there, is in my eye which is looking in the mirror. As Nietzsche says, "He who despises himself nevertheless esteems himself as a despiser."

For the tragic hero suffering is real and destructive; for the comic hero it is unreal or temporary or curative; for both it is a sign that they are not in the truth: both suffer with misunderstanding. The saint, on the other hand, is ironically related to suffering; it is real, nevertheless he understands that it is a blessing, a sign that he is in the truth. "I say pain but ought to say solace."

The Knight Errant

The Knight Errant, whom Don Quixote wishes to become and actually parodies, was an attempt to christianize the pagan epic hero, i.e., the Knight Errant,

a) possesses epic *areté* of good birth, good looks, strength, etc.
b) This *areté* is put in the service of the law, to rescue the unfortunate, protect the innocent, and combat the wicked.
c) His motives are three: (i) the desire for glory.
                              (ii) the love of justice.
                              (iii) the love of an individual woman who judges and rewards.
d) He suffers exceptionally, first in his adventures and collisions with the lawless, secondly in his temptations to lawlessness in the form of unchastity and, thirdly, in his exceptionally difficult erotic romance.

e) In the end he succeeds in this world. Vice is punished, and
virtue is rewarded by the lady of his heart.

When we first meet Don Quixote he is (*a*) poor, (*b*) not a knight, (*c*)
fifty, (*d*) has nothing to do except hunt and read romances about Knight-
Errantry. Manifestly, he is the opposite of the heroes he admires, i.e., he is
lacking in the epic *areté* of birth, looks, strength, etc. His situation, in fact,
is aesthetically uninteresting except in one thing: his passion is great
enough to make him sell land to buy books. This makes him aesthetically
comic. Religiously he is tragic; for he is a hearer not a doer of the word, the
weak man guilty in his imagination of Promethean pride. Now suddenly he
goes mad, i.e., he sets out to become what he admires. Aesthetically this
looks like pride; in fact, religiously, it is a conversion, an act of faith, a
taking up of his cross.

The Quixotic Madness and the Tragic Madness

The tragic hero is tempted by an *areté* he possesses to conquer this
world, whose nature he knows. His decisions are the result of a calculation of
the probabilities of success, and each success increases his madness (e.g.,
Iago). Don Quixote is (*a*) lacking in *areté*, (*b*) has a fantastic conception of this
world, (*c*) always meets with failure yet is never discouraged, (*d*) suffers
himself intentionally and makes others suffer only unintentionally.

The Quixotic Madness and the Comic Madness

The comic rogue declares: The World = that which exists to give me
money, beauty, etc. I refuse to suffer by being thwarted. He is cured by being
forced to suffer through collision with the real world.

Don Quixote declares: The World = that which needs my existence to
save it at whatever cost to myself. He comes into collision with the real world
but insists upon continuing to suffer. He becomes the Knight of the Doleful
Countenance but never despairs.

Don Quixote and Hamlet

Hamlet lacks faith in God and in himself. Consequently he must define
his existence in terms of others, e.g., I am the man whose mother married his
uncle, who murdered his father. He would like to become what the Greek

tragic hero is, a creature of situation. Hence his inability to act, for he can
only "act," i.e., play at possibilities.

Don Quixote is the antithesis of an actor, being completely incapable
of seeing himself in a role. Defining his situation in terms of his own
character, he is completely unreflective.

Madness and Faith

To have faith in something or someone means:

a) that the latter is not manifest. If it becomes manifest, then
    faith is no longer required.
b) The relation of faith between subject and object is unique in
    every case. Hundreds may believe, but each has to believe
    by himself.

Don Quixote exemplifies both. (*a*) He never sees things that aren't there
(delusion) but sees them differently, e.g., windmills as giants, sheep as armies,
puppets as Moors, etc. (*b*) He is the only individual who sees them thus.

Faith and Idolatry

The idolater makes things out to be stronger than they really are so that
they shall be responsible for him, e.g., he might worship a windmill for its
giant-like strength. Don Quixote never expects things to look after him; on the
contrary he is always making himself responsible for things and people who
have no need of him and regard him as an impertinent old meddler.

Faith and Despair

People are tempted to lose faith (*a*) when it fails to bring worldly
success, (*b*) when the evidence of their senses and feelings seem against it.
Don Quixote (*a*) is constantly defeated yet persists, (*b*) between his fits of
madness sees that windmills are not giants but windmills, etc., yet, instead of
despairing, says, "Those cursed magicians delude me, first drawing me into
dangerous adventures by the appearances of things as they really are and then
presently changing the face of things as they please." His supreme test comes
when Sancho Panza describes a country wench, whom Don Quixote sees

correctly as such, as the beautiful Princess Dulcinea and in spite of his feelings concludes that he is enchanted and that Sancho Panza is right.

Don Quixote and the Knight Errant

Don Quixote's friends attack the Romances he loves on the grounds that they are historically untrue, and lacking in style.

Don Quixote, on the other hand, without knowing it, by his very failure to imitate his heroes exactly, at once reveals that the Knight Errant of the Romances is half-pagan, and becomes himself the true Christian Knight.

Epic Dualism

The world of the Romances is a dualistic world where the completely good and innocent fight the completely evil and guilty. The Knight Errant comes into collision only with those who are outside the law, giants, heretics, heathens, etc. Don Quixote when in one of his spells, under the illusion that he is showing the righteous anger of the Knight Errant, comes into collision with the law, i.e., he attacks innocent clerics and destroys other people's property.

When he is not deluded as to the nature of those he is trying to help, e.g., the convicts or the boy being thrashed, he only succeeds in making things worse and earns enmity, not gratitude.

Frauendienst

Don Quixote affirms all the articles of the Amor religion, namely, that (*a*) the girl must be noble and beautiful, (*b*) there must be some barrier, (*c*) the final goal of the Knight's trials is to be rewarded by having his love reciprocated.

In fact, the girl he calls Dulcinea del Toboso is "a good likely country lass for whom he had formerly had a sort of inclination, though 'tis believed she never heard of it." She is of lower social status, and he is past the age when sexual love means anything to him. Nevertheless, his behaviour has all the courage that might be inspired by a great passion.

Again, Don Quixote expects to be tempted to unchastity so that, in the inn when the hunchback maid is trying to reach the carter's bed, he fancies that she is the daughter of the Governor of the Castle, who has fallen in love with him and is trying to seduce him. Bruised and battered as he is, even Don Quixote has to admit that for the moment he has no capacity.

The language is the language of Eros, the romantic idolization of the fair woman, but its real meaning is the Christian Agape, which loves all equally irrespective of their merit.

Snobbery

The true Knight Errant has nothing to do with the Lower Orders and must never put himself in an undignified position, e.g., Launcelot is disgraced by riding in a cart. Don Quixote attempts to do likewise but with singular unsuccess. He is constantly having to do with the Lower Orders under the illusion that they are the nobility. His aristocratic refusal to pay, which he adopts out of literary precedence, not personal feeling, never works out—he ends by overpaying. Again the language is the language of the feudal knight, but the behaviour is that of the Suffering Servant. This may be compared with the reverse situation in *Moby Dick*, when Captain Ahab leaves his cabin boy in his captain's cabin and mounts the look-out like an ordinary seaman: here the behaviour is apparently humble, but in fact the extremity of pride.

This-Worldliness

The Knight Errant is this-worldly in that he succeeds in arms and in love. Don Quixote professes a similar hope but in fact is not only persistently defeated but also cannot in the end even maintain in combat that Dulcinea is without a rival. Thus, he not only has to suffer the Knight's trials but also must suffer the consciousness of defeat. He is never able to think well of himself. He uses the language of the epic hero, but reveals himself to us as the Knight of Faith, whose kingdom is not of this world.

Sancho Panza and Don Quixote

Without his comic lymphatic squire, the Knight of the Doleful Countenance would be incomplete. Sancho Panza's official motive for following Don Quixote is the promise of a governorship. But this is a purely imaginary idea to the former, and in the end he reveals his motives, which are (*a*) for the excitement, (*b*) for love of his master. Sancho Panza sees the world that requires changing as it is, but has no wish himself to change it. Yet it turns out that he is the one who has to play the part of the Knight Errant and rescue his distressed master from misfortune. Don Quixote wishes to change the world but has no idea what the world is like. He fails to change anything except Sancho Panza's character. So the two are eternally related. Don Quixote needs Sancho Panza as the one creature about whom he has no illusions but loves as he is; Sancho Panza needs Don Quixote as the one constant loyalty in his life which is independent of feeling. Take away Don Quixote, and Sancho Panza is so nearly pure flesh, immediacy of feeling, so nearly without will that he becomes a hedonist pagan who rejects everything but matter. Take away Sancho Panza, on the other hand, and Don Quixote is so nearly pure spirit that he becomes a Manichee who rejects matter and feeling and is nothing but an egotistic will.

Don Quixote's Death

However many further adventures one may care to invent for Don Quixote—and, as in all cases of a true myth, they are potentially infinite—the conclusion can only be the one which Cervantes gives, namely, that he recovers his senses and dies. Despite the protestations of his friends, who want him to go on providing them with amusement, he must say: "Ne'er look for birds of this year in the nests of the last: I was mad, but I am now in my senses: I was once Don Quixote de la Mancha, but am now the plain Alonso Quixano, and I hope the sincerity of my words and my repentance may restore me the same esteem you have had for me before."

For, in the last analysis, the saint cannot be presented aesthetically. The ironic vision gives us a Don Quixote, who is innocent of every sin but one; and that one sin he can put off only by ceasing to exist as a character in a book, for all such characters are condemned to it, namely, the sin of being at all times and under all circumstances interesting.

Analogy is not identity.

Art is not enough.

VLADIMIR NABOKOV

Cruelty and Mystification

I now plan to tackle the mystification theme, the cruelty theme. This is how I am going to proceed. First of all, I am going to pass in review samples of cheerful physical cruelty in part one of the book. Remember that my complete account of Don Quixote's victories and defeats will come much later: I want you to look forward to that play-by-play account. So for the present all I shall do is to illume a corner of the torture house by means of my little torchlight, and this is the first thing I shall do today—samples of cheerful physical cruelty in part one. Secondly I shall discuss the mental cruelties of part two; and since these mental cruelties are mainly mystification, I shall have to speak of the various enchantments and enchanters. Our first enchanter will be Sancho—and this will introduce the Dulcinea theme. Another interesting case will be Don Quixote in an act of self-enchantment—the Montesinos cave episode. After that I shall be ready to attack the principal enchanters of the second part, the Duchess and her Duke.

I feel that there is something about the ethics of our book that casts a livid laboratory light on the proud flesh of some of its purpler passages. We are going to speak of cruelty.

The author seems to plan it thus: Come with me, ungentle reader, who enjoys seeing a live dog inflated and kicked around like a soccer football;

From *Lectures on Don Quixote*. © 1983 by the Estate of Vladimir Nabokov.

reader, who likes, of a Sunday morning, on his way to or from church, to poke his stick or direct his spittle at a poor rogue in the stocks; come, ungentle reader, with me and consider into what ingenious and cruel hands I shall place my ridiculously vulnerable hero. And I hope you will be amused at what I have to offer.

It is simply not true that as some of our mellow-minded commentators maintain—Aubrey Bell, for instance—that the general character that emerges from the national background of the book is that of sensitive, keen-witted folks, humorous and humane. Humane, indeed! What about the hideous cruelty—with or without the author's intent or sanction—which riddles the whole book and befouls its humor? Let us not drag the national element in. The Spaniards of Don Quixote's day were not more cruel in their behavior toward madmen and animals, subordinates and non-conformers, than any other nation of that brutal and brilliant era. Or, for that matter, of other, later, more brutal and less brilliant eras in which the fact of cruelty remains with its fangs bared. That the rustler in the chain gang which Don Quixote meets on the road had been given the rack is mentioned as a matter of course, for torture was as generously—though more openly—applied in old Spain or old Italy as it is in our time in totalitarian states. In Don Quixote's day Spaniards thought insanity comic but (as Krutch points out) so did the Englishmen of a later date who used to make visits of pleasure to Bedlam.

Both parts of *Don Quixote* form a veritable encyclopedia of cruelty. From that viewpoint it is one of the most bitter and barbarous books ever penned. And its cruelty is artistic. The extraordinary commentators who talk through their academic caps or birettas of the humorous and humane mellowly Christian atmosphere of the book, of a happy world where "all is sweetened by the humanities of love and good fellowship," and particularly those who talk of a certain "kindly duchess" who "entertains the Don" in the second Part—these gushing experts have probably been reading some other book or are looking through some rosy gauze at the brutal world of Cervantes's novel. There is a legend that one sunny morning King Philip the Third of Spain (a freak in his own right, who had succeeded in 1598 his father, the gloomy and fish-cold Philip the Second) upon looking from the balcony of his palace was struck by the singular behavior of a young student who was sitting on a bench in the shade of a cork oak (*quercus suber*) with a book and frantically clapping his thigh and giving vent to wild shrieks of laughter. The king remarked that the fellow was either crazy or was reading *Don Quixote*. A rapid courtier ran out to find the answer. The fellow, as you have guessed, was reading *Don Quixote*.

What exactly provoked this outburst of wild merriment in the gloomy world of the Philips? I have listed a whole set of jollities for the merry young student to choose from. Remember, I am looking at the book today only from this special viewpoint; there are many other things in our knight's adventures of which I shall talk later. So we start in chapter 3 with the innkeeper who allows a haggard madman to stay at his inn just in order to laugh at him and have his guests laugh at him. We go on with a shriek of hilarity to the half-naked lad flogged with a belt by a hefty farmer (chapter 4). We are convulsed with laughter again in chapter 4 when a mule driver pounds the helpless Don Quixote like wheat in a mill. In chapter 8 another belly laugh is given unto us by the servants of some traveling monks, who pull every hair from Sancho's beard and kick him mercilessly. What a riot, what a panic! Some carriers in chapter 15 beat Rocinante so hard that he drops to the ground half-dead—but never mind, in a minute the puppet master will revive his squeaking dolls.

If Don Quixote is not actually administered an enema of snow water and sand, as one of the characters in a book of chivalry was, he gets very close to it. Attitudes of excruciating pain such as that of Sancho Panza in the same chapter 15 provoke another moan of mirth. By this time Don Quixote has lost half an ear—and nothing can be funnier than losing half an ear except of course losing three-quarters of an ear—and now, please, notice the blows that he received during one day and one night: (1) wallops with packstaves, (2) a punch on the jaw at the inn, (3) sundry blows in the dark, (4) a bang on the pate with an iron lantern. And the next day is nicely started by his losing most of his teeth when stoned by some shepherds. The fun becomes positively rollicking by chapter 17 when in the famous blanket-tossing scene, some artisans—woolcombers and needlemakers, described as "merry fellows all of them, well intentioned, mischievous, and playful"—amuse themselves at Sancho's expense by tossing him in a blanket as men do with dogs at Shrovetide—a casual allusion to humane and humorous customs. The young student whom King Philip observes is again convulsed as he reads in chapter 18 of Don Quixote and Sancho vomiting over each other. And what fun there is in the scene of the galley slaves in chapter 22—another famous episode. Don Quixote asks one of the men for what sins is he in this evil plight. Another answers for him: "'This one, sir,' he said, 'is going as a canary—I mean, as a musician and singer.'" What, says Don Quixote, "do musicians and singers go to the galleys too?" The galley slave replied, "'Yes, sir; and there is nothing worse than singing when you're in trouble.'

"'On the contrary,' said Don Quixote, 'I have heard it said that he who sings frightens away his sorrows.'

"'It is just the opposite,' said the prisoner, 'for he who sings once weeps all his life long.'

"'I do not understand,' said the knight.

"One of the guards then explained. 'Sir Knight, with this *non sancta* tribe, to sing when you're in trouble means to confess under torture. This sinner was put to the torture and confessed his crime, which was that of being a *cuatrero*, or cattle thief, and as a result of his confession he was condemned to six years in the galleys in addition to two hundred lashes which he took on his shoulders; and so it is he is always downcast and moody, for the other thieves, those back where he came from and the ones here, mistreat, snub, ridicule, and despise him for having had confessed and for not having had the courage to deny his guilt. They are in the habit of saying that the word *no* has the same number of letters as the word *si*, and that a culprit is in luck when his life or death depends on his own tongue and not that of witnesses or upon evidence; and, in my opinion, they are not very far wrong.'" This is the humorous and humane world of some of our mellower Cervantesists.

Let us pursue our inquiry into the young student's mirth. Physical cruelty is of course fun, but mental cruelty may be still more amusing. In chapter 30 there is a charming young lady, Dorotea, a great favorite with Cervantesists; and of course she was too quick and intelligent not to understand what delightful possibilities Don Quixote's madness contained, so that seeing that everyone was making fun of him she was anxious not to be left out. Anxious not to be left out. Wise, lovely, winsome Dorotea!

We are back at the enchanted inn, or *venta*, in chapter 43, and there is another scene that is supposed to tickle the readers pink. Don Quixote stands upon the saddle of his horse to reach the barred window at which he imagines a lovelorn damsel is standing—and the servant girl, who impersonates her, ties his hand with the halter of Sancho's donkey in such a way that, when his horse moves, Don Quixote is left suspended, in which position he remains for two hours, despairing, bewildered, and bellowing like a bull, while the maid servant and the innkeeper's daughter, and presumably millions of readers, are doubled up with laughter, as probably were many in the crowd sixteen centuries earlier when the martyred God of those people was given vinegar instead of water.

The episodes at the inn end in Don Quixote being tied up and put into a cage on an ox cart by his friends the curate and the barber, who want to bring him home and cure him of his madness. We come now to a last fight in the first part. This is in chapter 52. While carting Don Quixote home, the curate falls into conversation with a learned and amiable canon, and they sit down for a picnic beside the road and have Don Quixote come out of his cage to join them in order to amuse them, to have sport with him as the saying went. During this picnic Don Quixote gets involved in a quarrel with a passing goatherd, whom he hits in the face with a loaf of bread. The goatherd tries to choke Don Quixote, but Sancho comes to the rescue by throwing the goatherd onto the tablecloth and upsetting or smashing everything upon it. Don Quixote endeavors to get on top of the goatherd, who, with his face all bloody from Sancho's kicks, is groping for a knife on the tablecloth.

Now keep an eye on the good canon, the good curate, and the good barber, remembering that the canon is Cervantes himself in disguise as a member of the clergy and remembering that the curate and the barber are Don Quixote's closest friends and are anxious to cure him of his madness. The canon and the curate prevent the goatherd from using a knife, but the barber helps the goatherd to get Don Quixote down again where he rains such a shower of blows on him that the knight's face poured blood as freely as the goatherd's. The barber is doing this, I suppose, for fun's sake. Now keep an eye on the others. The canon and the curate are bursting with laughter; the troopers of the highway patrol dance for joy—and everyone cheers the fighters on as men do at a dogfight. It is on this familiar dog note— nothing funnier than a dog being tortured in a sunny street—it is on this note that the first part of *Don Quixote* ends. Our young student is by now limp with laughter, has, in fact, fallen off his bench. We shall leave him lying there, although there is still a second part to read with more screams of merriment.

Let none think, however, that the symphony of mental and physical pain presented in *Don Quixote* is a composition that could be played only on musical instruments of the remote past. Nor should anyone suppose that those strings of pain are twanged nowadays only in remote tyrannies behind iron curtains. Pain is still with us, around us, among us. I am not referring to such trivialities—though they also have their place in the history of pain—as the banged heads and kicked groins and punched noses that are such delectable features of our movies and comics. What I have in mind are more trivial things, under the best of governments. Now and then freakish children in our schools are still tortured by their comrades as thoroughly as Childe Quixote was tortured by his enchanters; and now and then bums, colored and white, are as lustily kicked in the shins by burly policemen as the armored tramp and his squire were on the roads of Spain.

But let us turn to the second part of our humane, humorous book. Compared to the fun of the first part, the mirth-provoking cruelty of the second part reaches a higher and more diabolical level in regard to the mental forms it takes and sinks to a new low of incredible crudity in its physical aspect. The mystification theme becomes more prominent; enchantments and enchanters swarm. It is under their colors that I intend to wander through the second part. They had of course been present in the first part—Sancho himself had mystified his master when he carried a garbled message to a nonexisting Dulcinea. In fact, the trick was quite subtle since he lied and deceived his master not by saying he had seen Dulcinea the princess, but by saying he had seen the Tobosan girl Aldonza, whom actually he had not bothered to see. We shall thus mark that it is Sancho in the first part who starts the trend of Dulcinea's enchantment, her transformation from princess into a particular or generalized peasant wench.

The second part opens with Sancho trying his hand at a second act of enchantment on the same lines. He manages to persuade his master—by now his victim—that one of three peasant girls they meet (none of whom is Aldonza) is Dulcinea transformed.

At the end of chapter 8 of the second part they reach El Toboso. Don Quixote's purpose is to find Dulcinea there. Both knight and squire are secretly worried about her. The Don because a very vague, very secret doubt is forming cloudlike in the otherwise limpid heavens of his madness; and the squire because he has never seen her but has deceived his master into thinking he transmitted a letter to her, in the first part. In the next chapter there is a stumbling search in the dark for a palace in a back alley. Sancho suggests that Don Quixote hide in a forest while he goes to find Dulcinea. It was a device of genius to keep Dulcinea out of the first part. Will Cervantes produce her now?

As in the first part Don Quixote now sends Sancho with a message to Dulcinea, a message that Sancho again does not deliver. There is in chapter 10 a lovely paragraph: "'Go, my son,' Don Quixote said to him, 'and do not let yourself be dazed by the light from that sun of beauty that you go to seek. Ah, happy are you above all the squires in the world! Be sure to remember, and do not let it slip your mind, just how she receives you. Note whether she changes color while you are giving her my message and if she is restless and perturbed upon hearing my name. It may be that you will find her seated in sumptuous and royal state, in which case she will perhaps fall back upon a cushion; or if she be standing, see if she rests first upon one foot then upon the other. Observe if she repeats two or three times the answer she gives you and if her mood varies from mildness to austerity, from the harsh to the amorous. She may raise a hand to smooth it back, though it be not disordered.'" (A charming detail, this.)

Sancho comes riding back. He sees three peasant girls riding and now decides what to do. Hastening back to Don Quixote he finds the knight sighing and uttering amorous laments.

"'What is it, Sancho, my friend? Am I to be able to mark this day with a white stone or a black one?'

"'It would be better,' replied Sancho, 'if your Grace marked it with red ocher like the lists on the professors' chairs [of bachelors qualifying for degrees], so that all could see it very plainly.'

"'That means, I take it,' said Don Quixote, 'that you bring good news.'

"'Good news it is,' replied Sancho. 'All your Grace has to do is put spur to Rocinante and ride out into the open, and there you will see the lady Dulcinea del Toboso in person, who with two of her damsels has come to pay her respects to your Grace.

"'. . . She and her damsels are all one blaze of gold, pearls, diamonds, rubies, and brocade cloth with more than ten borders. Their hair falling loose over their shoulders are so many sunbeams playing with the wind.'"

Don Quixote hastens out of the wood but at the moment of encounter a curious sadness, a very real sadness, hangs over him as if suddenly, at this crucial moment, an awful doubt arises in him: Does Dulcinea exist? "'I see nothing,' declared Don Quixote, 'except three farm girls on three jackasses.'" Nevertheless, with Sancho, he falls on his knees before her. "His eyes were fairly starting from their sockets and there was a deeply troubled look in them as he stared up at the one whom Sancho had called queen and lady; all that he could see in her was a village wench, and not a very pretty one at that, for she was round-faced and snub-nosed. He was astounded and perplexed and did not dare open his mouth." But urged by Sancho he comes to believe that this girl, smelling of raw garlic, with dull red hair and a bristly mole at the corner of her lips, is Dulcinea under the spell of a wicked enchanter. He addresses her: "And thou, who art all that could be desired, the sum of human gentleness and sole remedy for this afflicted heart that doth adore thee! The malign enchanter who doth persecute me hath placed clouds and cataracts upon my eyes, and for them and them alone hath transformed thy peerless beauty into the face of a lowly peasant maid; and I can only hope that he has not likewise changed my face into that of some monster by way of rendering it abhorrent in thy sight. But for all of that, hesitate not to gaze upon me tenderly and lovingly, beholding in this act of submission as I kneel before thee a tribute to thy metamorphosed beauty from this humbly worshiping heart of mine."

Thinking she was being made fun of, the wench addressed as Dulcinea prodded her donkey with a spiked stick with the result that she was thrown to the ground by the animal's capers. "When he saw this, Don Quixote hastened to lift her up while Sancho busied himself with tightening the girths and adjusting the packsaddle, which had slipped down under the animal's belly. This having been accomplished, Don Quixote was about to take his enchanted lady in his arms to place her upon the she-ass when the girl saved him the trouble by jumping up from the ground, stepping back a few paces, and taking a run for it. Placing both hands upon the crupper of the ass, she landed more lightly than a falcon upon the packsaddle and remained sitting there astride it like a man.

"'In the name of Roque!' exclaimed Sancho, 'our lady is like a lanner, only lighter, and can teach the cleverest Cordovan or Mexican how to mount. She cleared the back of the saddle in one jump, and without any spurs she makes her hackney run like a zebra, and her damsels are not far behind, for they all of them go like the wind.'"

Henceforth throughout the second part Don Quixote will be worrying about how to accomplish the disenchantment of Dulcinea: how to transform the ugly peasant wench back into the beautiful Dulcinea, whom he vaguely remembers as another peasant girl, a handsome one, in El Toboso.

Another type of deception: The curate and the barber agree to the bachelor's suggestion that he, Sanson Carrasco, should take the road as a knight-errant, pick up somewhere a quarrel with Don Quixote and overcome him in battle. Then he would bid him go home—and remain there for one or two years, or more. Unfortunately it so happens that it is the bachelor who is defeated and badly battered. Don Quixote rides off well satisfied.

From the point of view of the structure, the two deceptions—Sancho deceiving Don Quixote into thinking that Dulcinea is under a spell and the bachelor disguising himself as a knight-errant to meet Don Quixote on his own dream terms—these two deceptions are the two feet on which the whole second part must stand or stumble. From now on, whatever plot is unfolded it will do so against the background of Don Quixote's longing for the ultimate disenchantment of Dulcinea; while, on the other hand, the unfortunate Knight of the Mirrors, the badly battered bachelor, is expected to take the field again as soon as he can sit in a saddle. Thus the reader, while watching the various meanders of the story and the various characters that appear, is supposed to rely upon Dulcinea appearing and the bachelor disguising himself again when the author deems it necessary. The bachelor will fight again and be victor; Dulcinea will be disenchanted—but she will never appear.

We have now reached the episode of Montesinos's cave in part two, which I intend to discuss. I shall then analyze the ducal enchantments, the series of mystifications in the ducal castle. I shall draw your attention, finally, to a couple of great passages in the book—artistically redeeming it.

Montesinos is a character from the literature of chivalry, the protagonist of the so-called "Ballads of Montesinos." (A Welsh enchanter, Merlin, had tampered with some other characters of those ballads.) This curious episode is contained in chapters 22, 23, and the first pages of chapter 24; and various references to it are found in later chapters, with a kind of sequel to the whole affair in chapters 34 and 35 when the Duchess and Duke use the cave adventure, of which Don Quixote has told them, as a foundation for one of the elaborate mystifications of which they make Don Quixote a victim.

The episode of the cave of Montesinos has been called a compromise with reality. As an adventure it is unique in the book since it is a case not only of self-enchantment but of what appears to be deliberate self-enchantment on the part of our striped madman. We are never quite sure whether Don Quixote is or is not aware that he has invented the whole episode, and the various allusions to his state of mind in this connection are very interesting. Don Quixote decides to investigate a vertical cave, possibly an old mine shaft if we wish to be realistic. The entrance is clogged with brambles and fig trees through which he slashes his way with his sword after having tied a thousand or more feet of rope around his waist. He lets himself down. Sancho and a certain young scholar pay out the rope. They have payed out a couple of hundred feet and then there is silence. Finally Don Quixote is pulled out in a blissful swoon. In chapter 23 he tells of the wonderful adventures that befell him in the cave. Among other marvels, he has seen there Dulcinea, still enchanted, running about with two other peasant girls—apparently a reflected image of the same trio that Sancho had produced in an earlier chapter. She behaves in his dream not like Princess Dulcinea, but as Aldonza the country girl, and indeed Don Quixote is rather flippant about the whole business. In the beginning of chapter 24 the chronicler of his history says that he cannot possibly suppose that Don Quixote had deliberately made up the whole thing and was lying—he who was the most truthful gentleman on earth. The episode adds a bizarre touch to Don Quixote's personality, and commentators have seen in the colored darkness of that cave a series of symbols relating to the very core of the question what is reality, what is truth. However, I am inclined to consider the episode as just another twist that Cervantes gives to the Enchanted Dulcinea theme in order to keep the reader entertained and Don Quixote busy. The problem now is how to disenchant Dulcinea. We now come to the main pair of villainous enchanters in the book, the Duchess and her Duke. The cruelty of the book reaches here atrocious heights. The ducal mystification theme occupies in all twenty-eight chapters and about 200 pages of the second part (chapters 30 to 57), and then an additional couple of chapters (69 and 70) deal with the same theme, after which there are only four chapters or about thirty pages to go to the end of the book. As I shall explain later, it is probable that the break, the gap of eleven chapters between the first set of chapters and the second set, is due to Cervantes having to deal in all haste with an enchanter in his own life, a mysterious writer who published a spurious *Second Volume of Don Quixote* while Cervantes was writing his own second part. The spurious continuation is first mentioned in chapter 59. Then Cervantes throws Don Quixote and Sancho back into the torture house.

So the whole ducal episode takes in all thirty chapters, almost a fourth of the whole work. The ducal theme starts in chapter 30 with Don Quixote and his squire emerging from a wood and seeing in the haze of a sunset a glittering group. Green seems to be the author's favorite color, and the beautiful huntress they now meet is dressed in green and rides a horse caparisoned in green. She has read the first part of the adventures of Don Quixote and she and her husband are anxious to meet its hero and have some good tigerish sport with him. This Diana (a Diabolical Diana, let it be noted at once) and her husband decide that they will humor Don Quixote in every way and that as long as he stays with them they will treat him as a knight-errant, with all the customary ceremonies as described in the books of chivalry; for they have read those books and are very fond of them, in a sleek, chop-licking way.

Don Quixote then rides up with his visor raised, and as he is about to dismount, Sancho comes alongside to hold his stirrup for him; but unfortunately, as he descends from his gray, the squire catches his foot in one of the ropes of his packsaddle in such a manner that he could not get it loose and is left hanging there with his face and chest on the ground—various symbols and parodies of the strappado torture, hoisting and dropping the subject by means of ropes, are liberally scattered through the novel. "Now, Don Quixote was not used to dismounting without his stirrup being held, and, thinking that Sancho was already there to see to it, he threw himself off with a lurch, bringing with him Rocinante's saddle, which must have been poorly fastened, and, as a result, both he and the saddle came tumbling to the earth. Needless to say, he was very much ashamed and could only mutter curses between his teeth at the unfortunate Sancho, who still had his feet in the stocks." Poor Don Quixote ought to have taken this for a warning and an omen; for this is the ominous beginning of a long and cruel series. But "The duke thereupon ordered his huntsmen to assist the knight and squire, and they proceeded to lift Don Quixote, who was greatly shaken by his fall but who nonetheless, limping along as best he could, now came forward to kneel before the noble pair." His hosts are identified by one commentator as real people, the Duke and Duchess of Villahermosa, but this is just an example of the kind of human interest stuff that some Cervantesists delight in. Actually, the Diabolical Diana and her Duke are mere enchanters, invented by the master enchanter, Cervantes, and nothing else.

At the Duke's castle Don Quixote is given a great cloak of sumptuous scarlet cloth. (And I am singularly reminded of Another Martyr who was also given sumptuous clothes and called a King and jeered at by Roman soldiers.) This marvelous welcome greatly astonished Don Quixote; "indeed, it may be said that this was the first time that he really and wholly believed himself to be a true knight-errant and not a fanciful one, for here he was being treated in the very same manner as knights-errant in ages past, according to the storybooks he had read." He discourses at table and the ducal pair, the two smiling tigers, purr and plot.

Now Cervantes starts to weave an interesting pattern. There is going to be a double enchantment, two sets of spells which sometimes meet and mix, and sometimes run different ways. One series of spells are those that are planned in all detail by the ducal pair and more or less faithfully acted out by their servants. But sometimes the servants take the initiative, either to amaze and surprise their masters or because they just cannot fight off the temptation to play with the lean madman and the larded simpleton. At the meeting of the two spells the idiotic Duke and his feral Duchess are sometimes almost as aghast with wonder as if they had not thought up these or similar enchantments themselves. Never forget that the secret flaw in the Devil's might is stupidity. And once or twice the servants go too far and are rebuked and applauded at the same time. And finally the Diabolical Duchess takes an active physical part in the spells as we shall soon see.

The sequence of cruel pranks begins in chapter 32 with a solemn servant maid soaping the docile Don's face. This is the first joke thought up by the servants. Their masters are moved to anger and laughter, not knowing whether to punish the girls' "presumption" or reward them for the pleasure of seeing Don Quixote in that sorry state, soaped face and all. I suppose our friend, the young student-reader is again convulsed at this point. Then Sancho is tormented by the kitchen boys who try to wash his face in filthy sops, and the Duchess is shown dying with laughter. Thereafter Sancho is mockingly petted by her as a kind of court fool, and the Duke promises him the governorship of an island.

Don Quixote and Sancho had both been wary of spells, but now, without realizing it, they have fallen into the hands of enchanters—the Duke and the Duchess! "Great was the pleasure which the duke and duchess found," says our text, "in the conversation of Don Quixote and Sancho Panza, and being more anxious than ever to play a few jokes upon them that would have all the appearance of adventures," they seized upon the earlier episode in which Don Quixote had explored the deep shaft of a cave and had had a marvelous dream in its depths. The Duchess and Duke now decide to take what the knight had told them concerning this Cave of Montesinos as their starting point in perpetrating a hoax that should be truly out of the ordinary. Notice that whatever spells Sancho had been able to weave are now drowned in the general enchantment; and what tickles the Duchess especially is Sancho's vast simplicity, for he has come to believe that Dulcinea *has* been enchanted though he himself had plotted the whole business, as we know.

And so, a week later, having instructed the servants in everything that was expected of them, they proceed to take Don Quixote on a hunting expedition with as large a retinue of huntsmen and beaters as if he were a king. Sancho comes to grief, but Don Quixote hunts splendidly, attacking a huge boar which he and the others kill. Then comes the next hoax that the Duke and Duchess play on him. There is a kind of haze in the air that is a great help to the Duke and Duchess in carrying out what they have in mind. A little after twilight, just as night is falling, it seems of a sudden as if the entire wood is on fire. (Remember, this is the sunset of Don Quixote's life that illumes everything with a gold-and-green weird glow.) A moment later, here, there, and everywhere, a countless number of trumpets and other martial instruments are heard, as if many troops of cavalry were passing by. Then come innumerable cries of the kind the Moors give when joining battle, mingled with the blare of trumpets and bugles, the roll of drums, creating a furious and continuous din. (I repeat: Note that as often as not the Duke and Duchess are ridiculously aghast at their own inventions either because of improvements by the servants or because they are lunatics in their own right.) In the midst of the general fear, silence falls upon them as a postilion dressed like a demon passes, playing upon a huge hollow horn. When questioned by the Duke, "'I am the devil,' replied the courier in a horrendous voice. 'I come to see Don Quixote de la Mancha. Those whom you see here are six troops of enchanters who are bringing with them in a triumphal car the peerless Dulcinea del Toboso. She is under a magic spell and is accompanied by the gallant Frenchman, Montesinos. They come to inform Don Quixote as to how she, the said lady, may be disenchanted.'"

Dulcinea shall be restored to Don Quixote if—now comes the rib-splitting joke—if Sancho consents to take 3,000 lashes on his bare behind. Otherwise, says the Duke when he hears of the requirement, you do not get your island. The whole thing is very medieval, coarse, and stupid fun, as all fun that comes from the devil. Authentic humor comes from the angels. "The duke and duchess now returned to their castle with the object of following up the jest which had thus begun, as there was no serious occupation that gave them greater pleasure than this." This is the gist of all these ducal chapters—chop-licking satisfaction with a joke and the immediate planning of another just as brutal.

I shall not stop at the episode of the Distressed Duenna (chapters 36-41) beyond saying that two lovers, according to her story, were transformed into an ape and a crocodile by an enchanter Malambruno, and "These two rash lovers shall not regain their former shape until the valiant Manchegan shall come to meet me [Malambruno] in singlehanded encounter, since it is for his great valor alone that the fates have reserved this unheard-of adventure." There is the description of the Flying Horse that will carry Don Quixote to the remote kingdom of Candaya where those lovers are. "This steed is guided by means of a peg that he has in his forehead, which serves as a bridle, and he goes through the air at such a speed that it seems as if the very devils themselves must be carrying him.

" . . . Malambruno, through his arts, contrived to get possession of him and employs him in the journeys which he is all the time making here and there throughout the world. He is here today and tomorrow in France, and the next day in Potosi and the best of it is, this horse neither eats nor sleeps nor does he have to be shod. Without wings, he ambles through the air so smoothly that his rider can carry a cup full of water in his hand without spilling a single drop. . . ." This is an old theme. Similar flying machines are found in the *Arabian Nights*, also with a guiding peg in the neck.

The Distressed Duenna and her other female servants have also been enchanted and have magically grown beards, and they will be unbearded if Don Quixote is successful in disenchanting the lovers. The theme of the beard plays a curious part in the book (recall the washing of the beards in the beginning of the ducal episode) and it seems to have started from the initial allusions to shaving in part one—all that concern with barbers and with Don Quixote's helmet which was a barber's basin.

The wooden horse Clavileño is brought out, Don Quixote and Sancho (the latter under protest) mount and are blindfolded. "The knight tried the peg, and no sooner had he laid hands upon it than the duennas and all the others there present began calling out to them, 'God guide you, valiant knight! God be with you, intrepid squire! Now, now, you are going through the air, swifter than a dart! Already those below are gazing up at you in astonishment!'" Don Quixote and Sancho converse as they think they fly through the air, although actually their mount stands motionless on the ground. The knight admonishes Sancho: "'Do not squeeze me so much or you will throw me off. There is really no reason for you to be disturbed or frightened, for I can swear that in all the days of my life I never had an easier-going mount. It is as if we never stirred from one spot. Banish all fear, my friend, for the truth is, everything is going as it should and we have the wind to our poop.'

"'So we do,' replied Sancho. 'On this side, it's as strong as if they were blowing me on with a thousand pairs of bellows.'

"This was the truth, for a number of large bellows were producing the breeze in question. The whole adventure had been so thoroughly planned by the duke and duchess and their major-domo that not a single essential detail was lacking to make it perfect.

"'Without any doubt, Sancho,' remarked Don Quixote as he felt the puff, 'we must have reached the second aerial region, where the snow and hail are produced; it is in the third region that the thunder and lightning are engendered, and if we keep on ascending at this rate, we shall soon be in the region of fire. I do not know how to control the peg to keep us from mounting so high that the flames will scorch us.'

"Even as he said this they felt a warmth upon their faces, which came from pieces of tow, easy to ignite and to extinguish, suspended from the end of a reed held at some distance from them. . . .

"The entire conversation of the two brave horsemen was heard by the duke and duchess, who were extremely amused by it; and, wishing to put a finishing touch to this extraordinary and well-planned adventure, they now set fire to Clavileño's tail with some bits of tow, whereupon the horse, which was filled with detonating rockets, at once blew up with a loud noise, hurling Don Quixote and Sancho Panza to the ground half-scorched." It is then announced that merely by undertaking the adventure, Don Quixote has satisfied the requirements, and Malambruno has released the pair of lovers, and the bearded duennas, from his spell on orders from Merlin. Idiotic—the whole affair. In a word, the ducal castle is a kind of laboratory where two poor souls, Don Quixote and Sancho, are vivisected.

In chapter 42 "The duke and duchess were so well pleased with the successful and amusing outcome of the adventure of the Distressed One that they made up their minds to continue with the jest, seeing what a suitable subject they had when it came to accepting the imaginary for the real. Accordingly, having instructed their servants and vassals as to how to behave toward Sancho in the government of his promised island, they informed the squire the next day . . . that he was to make ready to go and assume his gubernatorial duties, as his islanders were waiting for him as for the showers of May." Don Quixote advises Sancho as to how to conduct himself in office. His directions are quite commonplace, and are modeled on similar noble and wise instructions in ancient books; but it is curious to contrast the mercy he speaks of in his advice on how to govern with the merciless behavior of his tormentors. Sancho enters upon his governorship, a village of about a thousand inhabitants, one of the best in the Duke's domain, with a wall around it. Relying on his good memory, he proves himself to be quite a Solomon in his judgments.

I shall divert for a moment the current of my study of the ducal enchantments to direct your attention to a point of great art. I think Cervantes felt that he was taking the line of least resistance—and suddenly the story develops a very special pair of very special wings. Art has a way of transcending the boundaries of reason. I wish to submit the following point:

this novel would have died of the laughter its picaresque plot was meant to provoke had it not contained episodes and passages that gently usher or sweep the reader into the dreamworld of permanent and irrational art. So— in part two, around chapter 40 of the book, Sancho at last gets his island. Chapters 42 and 43 treat of the advice that Don Quixote gives Sancho before the latter sets out to govern his island. Well does Don Quixote know how inferior the squire is to him, but his inferior is successful; he, the master, is not only denied his ultimate dream, the disenchantment of Dulcinea, but he has entered upon a strange decline. He knows fear. He knows the gloom of poverty. While plump Sancho is getting his rich island, lean Quixote is still in the same situation as he was when he started on the long and—in retrospect—dreary and inept sequence of his adventures. The main, if not the only, interest of his instructions to Sancho (as a fine Spanish commentator Madariaga has suggested to me) is that these instructions are but a means of raising himself in his own esteem above his successful inferior.

Don Quixote, it should be borne in mind, is the maker of his own glory, the only begetter of these marvels; and within his soul he carries the most dread enemy of the visionary: the snake of doubt, the coiled consciousness that his quest is an illusion. There is something in the tone of those instructions of his to Sancho that evokes in one the image of an elderly, seedy, obscure poet, who has never been successful in anything, giving to his sturdy, popular, extravert son a sound bit of advice as to how to be a prosperous plumber or politician. In chapter 44, which is the chapter I had in view when I alluded to the artistic dream element in the book, Sancho has been taken away to be governor and Don Quixote is left alone in that horrible ducal castle, a reality in comparison to his fancy, a castle where every turret conceals a claw, where every crenation is a fang. Reality out-Quixotes Quixote: Sancho is gone, and Don Quixote is strangely alone. There is a sudden lull, a melancholy and deep pause. Oh—I know, Cervantes makes haste to tell the reader, the ruder kind of reader—yes, reader, the funny fat squire, your favorite clown, has gone but "Meanwhile, listen to what happened to his master that same night, and if it does not make you laugh, it will at least cause you to part your lips in an apelike grin; for Don Quixote's adventures are to be greeted either with astonishment or with mirth." As a matter of fact, the anthropoid reader is apt to skip the all-important passage that I am now coming to, and is apt to skip it in order to get quickly to the so-called sidesplitting but in reality atrocious and brutal and fundamentally foolish episode of the cats.

Sancho has gone and Don Quixote is strangely alone and suddenly feels himself permeated with a strange sense of loneliness and yearning, something more than merely a sense of solitude, a kind of purposeless nostalgic longing. He retires to his room, declines any servant to enter, and having locked the door proceeds to undress by the light of two wax candles. He is alone but the curtains are, as it were, not drawn over the window of the story and we see through the window bars the gleam of the bright green stockings he is slowly shedding and studying—just as in reading another famous story, where the grotesque and the lyrical are somewhat similarly interwoven, Gogol's *Dead Souls*, we shall glimpse in the middle of the night a bright window and the glossy leather of a pair of new boots that a dreaming lodger admires without end.

But Don Quixote's stockings are anything but new. O disaster, the narrator sighs as he contemplates the bursting of several stitches in the left stocking which now has the appearance of a piece of lattice work. The wretched sense of poverty mingles with his general dejection and he finally goes to bed, moody and heavy-hearted. Is it only Sancho's absence and the burst threads of his stockings that induce this sadness, this Spanish *soledad*, this Portuguese *saudades*, this French *angoisse*, this German *sehnsucht*, this Russian *toska*? We wonder—we wonder if it does not go deeper. Remember that Sancho, his squire, is the crutch of Quixote's madness, the prop of his delusion, and now Don Quixote is strangely alone. He puts out the candles, but it is a very warm night and he cannot sleep. Rising from his bed Don Quixote partly opens the grated window and looks out on a moon-charmed garden and becomes aware of feminine voices conversing—especially the voice of Altisidora, the Duchess's maid, a young girl, a child, who in the scheme of atrocious cruelty governing this and other scenes, poses as a lovelorn maiden passionately attached to La Mancha's bravest knight.

As he stands at the grated window, there comes the sound of a string instrument gently plucked; whereupon Don Quixote is deeply moved. His yearning, his loneliness, are resolved now in that twang of music, in that twinge of beauty. The inward hint, the veiled suspicion that Dulcinea may not exist at all, is now brought to light by contrast with a real melody, with a real voice; the real voice deceives him, of course, as much as his dream of Dulcinea does—but at least it belongs to a real damsel, and a charming one, and not to Maritornes, the homely whore of part one. He is deeply moved because at that moment all the innumerable adventures of a like sort—barred windows, gardens, music, and lovemaking—all he has read of in those now strangely true books of chivalry—come back to him with a new impact, his dreams mingling with reality, his dreams fertilizing reality. And the voice of the little damsel Altisidora (with the rolling R of Reality) so close at hand, in the garden, becomes for a moment, physically and mentally, more vivid than the vision of Dulcinea del Toboso, with all those limp, lisping l's of lean illusion. But his innate modesty, his purity, the glorious chastity of a true knight-errant, all this proves stronger than his manly senses—and after listening to the song in the garden he bangs the window shut, and now even more gloomy than before—"as if," says Cervantes, "some dire misfortune had befallen him," he goes to bed, leaving the garden to the fireflies and to the moaning girl-music and leaving the rich island to his ruddy squire.

This is an admirable scene—one of those scenes that pander to the imagination and deliver more than they seem to contain: dreamy, longing, gaunt, with those threadbare emerald stockings of his that lie crumpled on the floor, and the grated window, now shut, and the warm Spanish night that henceforth for three centuries is to become the breeding place of romantic prose-and-verse in all languages, and fifty-year-old Quixote fighting one delusion by means of another delusion—melancholy, miserable, tempted, excited by little Altisidora's musical moans.

Back to the torture house. The next night Don Quixote asks for a lute and sings a song he has composed that is intended to discourage Altisidora by his fidelity to Dulcinea "when suddenly from a gallery directly above his window they let down a rope to which were attached more than a hundred bells, and then they emptied a large bag filled with cats that had bells of a smaller size fastened to their tails. And so great was the din of the bells and so loud the squalling of the felines that even though the duke and duchess were the ones who had thought up the joke, they still were startled by it all. As for Don Quixote, he was quaking with fear. As luck would have it, two or three of the cats came in through the window of his room, darting from side to side, and it was as though a legion of devils had been let loose there. As they ran about seeking a means of escape, they put out the candles that were burning in the chamber. . . .

"Getting to his feet, Don Quixote drew his sword and started slashing at the window grating as he shouted, 'Away with you, malign enchanters! Out with you, witching rabble! Know that I am Don Quixote de la Mancha, against whom your evil intentions are of no avail!'

"Turning on the cats that were rushing around the room, [Don Quixote] made many thrusts at them, but they dashed for the window and leaped out—all except one, which, finding itself thus belabored by Don Quixote's sword, sprang at his face and seized his nose with its claws and teeth, causing him to cry out with pain at the top of his voice. When they heard this, the duke and duchess, who suspected what the trouble was, ran to his room and opened the door with their master key, only to behold the poor knight struggling with all the strength that he had to pull the cat away from his face.

" . . . The cat, however, only growled and held on; but the duke finally pulled it off and tossed it out the window. Don Quixote's face was perforated like a sieve and his nose was not in very good shape; yet for all of that, he was very much displeased that they had not permitted him to finish the hard-fought battle with that scoundrelly enchanter." In still another session with his torturers, when Doña Rodriguez seeks his help to redress the wrongs done to her daughter, in the tumult in the darkness that follows he is pinched by the Duchess herself.

Meanwhile, Sancho governs his island wisely until his stage-enemies invade the town, the culminating trick that is going to be played on the unfortunate Sancho. Mark that the Duke and Duchess are not present at the torture, but derive all necessary pleasure from the account that is given them later. The supposed defenders of the town call on Sancho to arm himself and lead them. Frightened as he is, "Arm me, then, for Heaven's sake," said Sancho. Two large shields are tied with rope, one in front of and the other behind him so that he cannot bend or move, and he is told to lead the villagers. Then a battle is staged, which consists of everybody trampling him as he lies helpless on the floor. He faints when they finally unbind him. When he comes to himself, he asks what time it is and is told that it is already daylight, and they have been victorious. Without saying another word, he starts to dress himself amid profound silence as they all watch and wait to see why he should be in such a hurry to put his clothes on. This silence reminds one of young school bullies who have been tormenting a fat weak boy, and now in silence Sancho gets up, wipes his face. Then, too sore to walk fast, he slowly makes his way to the stable, followed by all those present. There he embraced his gray, talked to him tenderly, adjusted the packsaddle, without a word from any of the bystanders. Then with great pain and difficulty he climbed upon the gray's back and spoke to them: "Clear the way, gentlemen, and let me go back to my old freedom. Let me go look for my past life so that I may be resurrected from this present death"—an almost Proustian note. In this one scene Sancho reveals a dignity and a slow sadness comparable to the melancholy emotions of his master.

Chapter 57 begins: "By now Don Quixote had come to feel that it would be well for him to quit a life of idleness such as he was leading in the castle; for he believed he was doing a great wrong in depriving the outside world of his presence, by keeping himself shut up like this, and leisurely enjoying all the innumerable comforts and luxuries with which my lord and lady surrounded him as a knight-errant. It seemed to him that he would have to give an accounting to Heaven for this sloth and seclusion; and so it was that one day he begged permission of the ducal pair to take his leave. They granted his request, at the same time showing how very sorry they were to have him go." Some adventures on the road to Barcelona involve him with the great brigand Roque Guinart, who makes arrangements to pass the Don and Sancho on to friends in Barcelona who can have sport with them. They are met by Roque's friend Don Antonio Moreno; and as they are entering the city with him some small boys, forcing their way through the crowd, lift up the tails of Rocinante and the gray and insert a bunch of furze (a prickly plant). The animals begin leaping and rearing and toss their riders to the ground. Those will laugh at this who just love bucking horses in commercial rodeos—bucking nags fitted with special corrosive belly straps.

In Barcelona, another kindly enchanter takes care of Don Quixote. Don Antonio was "a gentleman of wealth and discernment who was fond of amusing himself in an innocent and kindly way. Having taken the knight into his house, he began casting about for some harmless means of bringing out his mad traits." The first thing he does, accordingly, is to have Don Quixote remove his armor, which leaves him clad only in his tight-fitting chamois doublet, after which he leads him out onto the balcony overlooking the city in order that the people gathered there, including the small boys, may have a look at him. And there Don Quixote stands, an ignoble show, with the boys gaping at his gaunt and melancholy figure—lacking only a crown of thorns. That afternoon they take him out riding in such a heavy greatcoat "which at that season of the year would have made ice itself sweat." On the back of it they sewed a piece of parchment with an inscription in large letters "This is the king—" sorry—"THIS IS DON QUIXOTE DE LA MANCHA." "From the moment they set out, the placard attracted the attention of all those who had come to behold the spectacle, and the knight for his part was astonished to find so many people gazing at him and calling him by name. Turning to Don Antonio, who rode alongside him, he said, 'Great are the prerogatives of knight-errantry, seeing that it makes the one who follows that calling known and famous in all parts of the earth. If you do not believe me, Señor Don Antonio, your Grace has but to observe the lads of this city, who, though they have never seen me, nevertheless recognize me.'"

Afterward, at a party, the clumsy and tired Don Quixote is made to dance by two mischievous ladies, and finally, exhausted and depressed, amid screams of mirth he sits down in the middle of the ballroom floor, and kindly Don Antonio, seeing no further fun can be squeezed out of the martyr, has his servants carry him off to bed.

But the Duke and Duchess are not through with Don Quixote and Sancho. In chapter 68 armed horsemen are sent out to bring them back for some more fun. They discover the dejected pair on a country road, and with threats and imprecations they carry the pair to a castle which the knight recognizes as the Duke's. The horsemen dismount, pick up Don Quixote and Sancho bodily, and carry them into a courtyard. "There nearly a hundred torches, fixed in their sockets, were flaring, while the adjoining galleries were illuminated by more than five hundred lamps. . . . In the middle of the courtyard a funeral mound about two yards high had been reared, completely covered by an enormous black velvet canopy, and on the steps leading up to it more than a hundred white wax tapers in silver candlesticks were shedding their glow. Upon this catafalque lay the lifeless body of a maiden, so lovely as to make even death itself seem beautiful. Her head rested upon a brocade pillow and was crowned with a plaited garland of sweet-smelling flowers of various sorts; her hands were folded over her bosom and between them was a bough of the yellow palm of victory." It is Altisidora, disguised as a dead or sleeping beauty.

After much pageantry, a song, and speeches by characters representing Rhadamanthus and Minos, it is revealed that Altisidora can be released from the enchantment and brought to life only if Sancho's face is slapped and pinched. Despite his protests, six duennas of the household march in, and on Don Quixote's request Sancho allows himself to be smacked in the face by the duennas and various members of the household, "but the thing he could not stand was the pinpricks. When it came to that, he rose from his chair with a show of anger and, seizing a lighted torch that stood near by, began laying about him among the duennas and all his other tormentors, crying, 'Away with you, ministers of Hell! I am not made of brass so that I do not feel such unusual torture as this!'

"Then it was that Altisidora, who must have been tired of lying on her back for so long a time, turned over on her side, beholding which, all the bystanders shouted, with one voice as it were, 'Altisidora is alive! Altisidora lives!' And Rhadamanthus commanded Sancho to forego his wrath, seeing that their purpose had now been achieved." As the knight and Sancho are sleeping that night, Cervantes remarks, behind the silk mask of his Arabic historian Cid Hamete, "it is his personal opinion that the jesters were as crazy as their victims and that the duke and duchess were not two fingers' breadth removed from being fools when they went to so much trouble to make sport of the foolish." The episode just related has for its chapter 69 heading, "Of the strangest and most extraordinary adventure that has befallen Don Quixote in the entire course of this great history." One is under the impression that the author thinks that the more pageantry there is on the stage, the more supers, costumes, lights, kings, queens, et cetera, the greater the adventure will seem to the reader (as to today's moviegoer).

There is one last deception. Sancho by lashing at trees in the dark makes his master believe that he is giving himself the flogging that will disenchant Dulcinea—that in fact the necessary number of lashes has been administered and that somewhere in the mist Dulcinea is now actually being disenchanted. A star, a flushed sky, a growing sense of victory, of achievement. I would like you to note that this flogging of the beech trees is performed by means of the same donkey's halter that was used for two previous enchantments—the spell Sancho cast on Rocinante in the episode in part one, chapter 20, just before the adventure of the fulling mills, and the suspension in chapter 43 of Don Quixote at the inn window by the servant girl Maritornes.

JORGE LUIS BORGES

Pierre Menard, Author of Don Quixote

The *visible* works left by this novelist are easily and briefly enumerated. It is therefore impossible to forgive the omissions and additions perpetrated by Madame Henri Bachelier in a fallacious catalogue that a certain newspaper, whose Protestant tendencies are no secret, was inconsiderate enough to inflict on its wretched readers—even though they are few and Calvinist, if not Masonic and circumcised. Menard's true friends regarded this catalogue with alarm, and even with a certain sadness. It is as if yesterday we were gathered together before the final marble and the fateful cypresses, and already Error is trying to tarnish his Memory. . . . Decidedly, a brief rectification is inevitable.

I am certain that it would be very easy to challenge my meager authority. I hope, nevertheless, that I will not be prevented from mentioning two important testimonials. The Baroness de Bacourt (at whose unforgettable *vendredis* I had the honor of becoming acquainted with the late lamented poet) has seen fit to approve these lines. The Countess de Bagnoregio, one of the most refined minds in the Principality of Monaco (and now of Pittsburgh, Pennsylvania, since her recent marriage to the international philanthropist Simon Kautsch who, alas, has been so slandered by the victims of his disinterested handiwork) has sacrificed to "truth and death" (those are her words) that majestic reserve which distinguishes her, and in an open letter

From *Ficciones*. © 1962 by Grove Press Inc. Translated by Anthony Bonner.

published in the magazine *Luxe* also grants me her consent. These authorizations, I believe, are not insufficient.

I have said that Menard's *visible* lifework is easily enumerated. Having carefully examined his private archives, I have been able to verify that it consists of the following:

a) A symbolist sonnet which appeared twice (with variations) in the magazine *La Conque* (the March and October issues of 1899).

b) A monograph on the possibility of constructing a poetic vocabulary of concepts that would not be synonyms or periphrases of those which make up ordinary language, "but ideal objects created by means of common agreement and destined essentially to fill poetic needs" (Nîmes, 1901).

c) A monograph on "certain connections or affinities" among the ideas of Descartes, Leibnitz and John Wilkins (Nîmes, 1903).

d) A monograph on the *Characteristica Universalis* of Leibnitz (Nîmes, 1904).

e) A technical article on the possibility of enriching the game of chess by means of eliminating one of the rooks' pawns. Menard proposes, recommends, disputes, and ends by rejecting this innovation.

f) A monograph on the *Ars Magna Generalis* of Ramón Lull (Nîmes, 1906).

g) A translation with prologue and notes of the *Libro de la invención y arte del juego del axedrez* by Ruy López de Segura (Paris, 1907).

h) The rough draft of a monograph on the symbolic logic of George Boole.

i) An examination of the metric laws essential to French prose, illustrated with examples from Saint-Simon (*Revue des langues romanes*, Montpellier, October, 1909).

j) An answer to Luc Durtain (who had denied the existence of such laws) illustrated with examples from Luc Durtain (*Revue des langues romanes*, Montpellier, December, 1909).

k) A manuscript translation of the *Aguja de navegar cultos* of Quevedo, entitled *La boussole des précieux*.

l) A preface to the catalogue of the exposition of lithographs by Carolus Hourcade (Nîmes, 1914).

m) His work, *Les problèmes d'un problème* (Paris, 1917), which takes up in chronological order the various solutions of the

famous problem of Achilles and the tortoise. Two editions of
this book have appeared so far; the second has as an epigraph
Leibnitz' advice "Ne craignez point, monsieur, la tortue,"
and contains revisions of the chapters dedicated to Russell
and Descartes.

n) An obstinate analysis of the "syntactic habits" of Toulet
(*N.R.F.*, March, 1921). I remember that Menard used to
declare that censuring and praising were sentimental
operations which had nothing to do with criticism.

o) A transposition into Alexandrines of *Le Cimetière marin* of
Paul Valéry (*N.R.F.*, January, 1928).

p) An invective against Paul Valéry in the *Journal for the
Suppression of Reality* of Jacques Reboul. (This invective, it
should be stated parenthetically, is the exact reverse of his
true opinion of Valéry. The latter understood it as such, and
the old friendship between the two was never endangered.)

q) A "definition" of the Countess of Bagnoregio in the "victorious
volume"—the phrase is that of another collaborator, Gabriele
d'Annunzio—which this lady publishes yearly to rectify the
inevitable falsifications of journalism and to present "to the
world and to Italy" an authentic effigy of her person, which
is so exposed (by reason of her beauty and her activities) to
erroneous or hasty interpretations.

r) A cycle of admirable sonnets for the Baroness de Bacourt
(1934).

s) A manuscript list of verses which owe their effectiveness to
punctuation.

Up to this point (with no other omission than that of some vague,
circumstantial sonnets for the hospitable, or greedy, album of Madame
Henri Bachelier) we have the *visible* part of Menard's works in chronological
order. Now I will pass over to that other part, which is subterranean,
interminably heroic, and unequalled, and which is also—oh, the possibilities
inherent in the man!—inconclusive. This work, possibly the most significant
of our time, consists of the ninth and thirty-eighth chapters of Part One of
Don Quixote and a fragment of the twenty-second chapter. I realize that such
an affirmation seems absurd; but the justification of this "absurdity" is the
primary object of this note.*

*I also had another, secondary intent—that of sketching a portrait of Pierre Menard.
But how would I dare to compete with the golden pages the Baroness de Bacourt tells
me she is preparing, or with the delicate and precise pencil of Carolus Hourcade?

Two texts of unequal value inspired the undertaking. One was that philological fragment of Novalis—No. 2005 of the Dresden edition—which outlines the theme of *total* identification with a specific author. The other was one of those parasitic books which places Christ on a boulevard, Hamlet on the Cannebière and Don Quixote on Wall Street. Like any man of good taste, Menard detested these useless carnivals, only suitable—he used to say— for evoking plebian delight in anachronism, or (what is worse) charming us with the primary idea that all epochs are the same, or that they are different. He considered more interesting, even though it had been carried out in a contradictory and superficial way, Daudet's famous plan: to unite in *one* figure, Tartarin, the Ingenious Gentleman and his squire. . . . Any insinuation that Menard dedicated his life to the writing of a contemporary *Don Quixote* is a calumny of his illustrious memory.

He did not want to compose another *Don Quixote*—which would be easy—but *the Don Quixote*. It is unnecessary to add that his aim was never to produce a mechanical transcription of the original; he did not propose to copy it. His admirable ambition was to produce pages which would coincide—word for word and line for line—with those of Miguel de Cervantes.

"My intent is merely astonishing," he wrote me from Bayonne on December 30th, 1934. "The ultimate goal of a theological or metaphysical demonstration—the external world, God, chance, universal forms—are no less anterior or common than this novel which I am now developing. The only difference is that philosophers publish in pleasant volumes the intermediary stages of their work and that I have decided to lose them." And, in fact, not one page of a rough draft remain to bear witness to this work of years.

The initial method he conceived was relatively simple: to know Spanish well, to re-embrace the Catholic faith, to fight against Moors and Turks, to forget European history between 1602 and 1918, and to *be* Miguel de Cervantes. Pierre Menard studied this procedure (I know that he arrived at a rather faithful handling of seventeenth-century Spanish) but rejected it as too easy. Rather because it was impossible, the reader will say! I agree, but the undertaking was impossible from the start, and of all the possible means of carrying it out, this one was the least interesting. To be, in the twentieth century, a popular novelist of the seventeenth seemed to him a diminution. To be, in some way, Cervantes and to arrive at *Don Quixote* seemed to him less arduous—and consequently less interesting—than to continue being Pierre Menard and to arrive at *Don Quixote* through the experiences of Pierre Menard. (This conviction, let it be said in passing, forced him to exclude the autobiographical prologue of the second part of *Don Quixote*. To include this prologue would have meant creating another personage—Cervantes—but it would also have meant presenting *Don Quixote* as the work of this personage and not of Menard. He naturally denied himself such an easy solution.) "My undertaking is not essentially difficult," I read in another part of the same letter. "I would only have to be immortal in order to carry it out." Shall I confess that I often imagine that he finished it and that I am reading *Don Quixote*—the entire work—as if Menard had conceived it? Several nights ago, while leafing through Chapter XXVI—which he had never attempted—I recognized our friend's style and, as it were, his voice in this exceptional phrase: *the nymphs of the rivers, mournful and humid Echo.* This effective combination of two adjectives, one moral and the other physical, reminded me of a line from Shakespeare which we discussed one afternoon:

> *Where a malignant and turbaned Turk . . .*

Why precisely *Don Quixote*, our reader will ask. Such a preference would not have been inexplicable in a Spaniard; but it undoubtedly was in a symbolist from Nîmes, essentially devoted to Poe, who engendered Baudelaire, who engendered Mallarmé, who engendered Valéry, who engendered Edmond Teste. The letter quoted above clarifies this point. "*Don Quixote*," Menard explains, "interests me profoundly, but it does not seem to me to have been—how shall I say it—inevitable. I cannot imagine the universe without the interjection of Edgar Allan Poe

> *Ah, bear in mind this garden was enchanted!*

or without the *Bateau ivre* or the *Ancient Mariner,* but I know that I am capable of imagining it without *Don Quixote.* (I speak, naturally, of my personal capacity, not of the historical repercussions of these works.) *Don Quixote* is an accidental book, *Don Quixote* is unnecessary. I can premeditate writing, I can write it, without incurring a tautology. When I was twelve or thirteen years old I read it, perhaps in its entirety. Since then I have reread several chapters attentively, but not the ones I am going to undertake. I have likewise studied the *entremeses,* the comedies, the *Galatea,* the exemplary novels, and the undoubtedly laborious efforts of *Pérsiles y Sigismunda* and the *Viaje al Parnaso.* . . . My general memory of *Don Quixote,* simplified by forgetfulness and indifference, is much the same as the imprecise, anterior image of a book not yet written. Once this image (which no one can deny me in good faith) has been postulated, my problems are undeniably considerably more difficult than those which Cervantes faced. My affable precursor did not refuse the collaboration of fate; he went along composing his immortal work a little *à la diable*, swept along by inertias of language and invention. I have contracted the mysterious duty of reconstructing literally his spontaneous work. My solitary game is governed by two polar laws. The first permits me to attempt variants of a formal and psychological nature; the second obliges me to sacrifice them to the 'original' text and irrefutably to rationalize this annihilation. . . . To these artificial obstacles one must add another congenital one. To compose *Don Quixote* at the beginning of the seventeenth century was a reasonable, necessary and perhaps inevitable undertaking; at the beginning of the twentieth century it is almost impossible. It is not in vain that three hundred years have passed, charged with the most complex happenings—among them, to mention only one, that same *Don Quixote*."

In spite of these three obstacles, the fragmentary *Don Quixote* of Menard is more subtle than that of Cervantes. The latter indulges in a rather coarse opposition between tales of knighthood and the meager, provincial reality of his country; Menard chooses as "reality" the land of Carmen during the century of Lepanto and Lope. What Hispanophile would not have advised Maurice Barrès or Dr. Rodríguez Larreta to make such a choice! Menard, as if it were the most natural thing in the world, eludes them. In his work there are neither bands of gypsies, conquistadors, mystics, Philip the Seconds, nor autos-da-fé. He disregards or proscribes local color. This disdain indicates a new approach to the historical novel. This disdain condemns *Salammbô* without appeal.

It is no less astonishing to consider isolated chapters. Let us examine, for instance, Chapter XXXVIII of Part One "which treats of the curious discourse that Don Quixote delivered on the subject of arms and letters." As is known, Don Quixote (like Quevedo in a later, analogous passage of *La hora de todos*) passes judgment against letters and in favor of arms. Cervantes was an old soldier, which explains such a judgment. But that the *Don Quixote* of Pierre Menard—a contemporary of *La trahison des clercs* and Bertrand Russell—should relapse into these nebulous sophistries! Madame Bachelier has seen in them an admirable and typical subordination of the author to the psychology of the hero; others (by no means perspicaciously) a *transcription* of *Don Quixote*; the Baroness de Bacourt, the influence of Nietzsche. To this third interpretation (which seems to me irrefutable) I do not know if I would dare add a fourth, which coincides very well with the divine modesty of Pierre Menard: his resigned or ironic habit of propounding ideas which were the strict reverse of those he preferred. (One will remember his diatribe against Paul Valéry in the ephemeral journal of the superrealist Jacques Reboul.) The text of Cervantes and that of Menard are verbally identical, but the second is almost infinitely richer. (More ambiguous, his detractors will say; but ambiguity is a richness.) It is a revelation to compare the *Don Quixote* of Menard with that of Cervantes. The latter, for instance, wrote (*Don Quixote*, Part One, Chapter Nine):

> . . . *la verdad, cuya madre es la historia, émula del tiempo, depósito de las acciones, testigo de lo pasado, ejemplo y aviso de lo presente, advertencia de lo por venir.*

> [. . . truth, whose mother is history, who is the rival of time, depository of deeds, witness of the past, example and lesson to the present, and warning to the future.]

Written in the seventeenth century, written by the "ingenious layman" Cervantes, this enumeration is a mere rhetorical eulogy of history. Menard, on the other hand, writes:

> . . . *la verdad, cuya madre es la historia, émula del tiempo, depósito de las acciones, testigo de lo pasado, ejemplo y aviso de lo presente, advertencia de lo por venir.*

> [. . . truth, whose mother is history, who is the rival of time, depository of deeds, witness of the past, example and lesson to the present, and warning to the future.]

History, *mother* of truth; the idea is astounding. Menard, a contemporary of William James, does not define history as an investigation of reality, but as its origin. Historical truth, for him, is not what took place; it is what we think took place. The final clauses—*example and lesson to the present, and warning to the future*—are shamelessly pragmatic.

Equally vivid is the contrast in styles. The archaic style of Menard—in the last analysis, a foreigner—suffers from a certain affectation. Not so that of his precursor, who handles easily the ordinary Spanish of his time.

There is no intellectual exercise which is not ultimately useless. A philosophical doctrine is in the beginning a seemingly true description of the universe; as the years pass it becomes a mere chapter—if not a paragraph or a noun—in the history of philosophy. In literature, this ultimate decay is even more notorious. "*Don Quixote*," Menard once told me, "was above all an agreeable book; now it is an occasion for patriotic toasts, grammatical arrogance and obscene deluxe editions. Glory is an incomprehension, and perhaps the worst."

These nihilist arguments contain nothing new; what is unusual is the decision Pierre Menard derived from them. He resolved to outstrip that vanity which awaits all the woes of mankind; he undertook a task that was complex in the extreme and futile from the outset. He dedicated his conscience and nightly studies to the repetition of a pre-existing book in a foreign tongue. The number of rough drafts kept on increasing; he tenaciously made corrections and tore up thousands of manuscript pages.* He did not permit them to be examined, and he took great care that they would not survive him. It is in vain that I have tried to reconstruct them.

I have thought that it is legitimate to consider the "final" *Don Quixote* as a kind of palimpsest, in which should appear traces—tenuous but not undecipherable—of the "previous" handwriting of our friend. Unfortunately, only a second Pierre Menard, inverting the work of the former, could exhume and rescuscitate these Troys. . . .

"To think, analyze and invent," he also wrote me, "are not anomalous acts, but the normal respiration of the intelligence. To glorify the occasional fulfillment of this function, to treasure ancient thoughts of others, to remember with incredulous amazement that the *doctor universalis* thought, is to confess our languor or barbarism. Every man should be capable of all ideas, and I believe that in the future he will be."

Menard (perhaps without wishing to) has enriched, by means of a new technique, the hesitant and rudimentary art of reading: the technique is one of deliberate anachronism and erroneous attributions. This technique, with its infinite applications, urges us to run through the *Odyssey* as if it were written after the *Aeneid*, and to read *Le jardin du Centaure* by Madame Henri Bachelier as if it were by Madame Henri Bachelier. This technique would fill the dullest books with adventure. Would not the attributing of *The Imitation of Christ* to Louis Ferdinand Céline or James Joyce be a sufficient renovation of its tenuous spiritual counsels?

---

*I remember his square-ruled notebooks, the black streaks where he had crossed out words, his peculiar typographical symbols and his insect-like handwriting. In the late afternoon he liked to go for walks on the outskirts of Nîmes; he would take a notebook with him and make a gay bonfire.

MARK VAN DOREN

Don Quixote's Profession

A gentleman of fifty, with nothing to do, once invented for himself an occupation. Those about him, in his household and his village, were of the opinion that no such desperate step was necessary. He had an estate, and he was fond of hunting; these, they said, were occupation enough, and he should be content with the uneventful routines it imposed. But the gentleman was not content. And when he set out in earnest to live an altogether different life he was thought by everybody, first at home and then abroad, to be either strange or mad. He went away three times, returning once of his own accord but in the second and third cases being brought back by persons of the village who had pursued him for this purpose. He returned each time in an exhausted state, for the occupation he embraced was strenuous; and soon after his third homecoming he took to bed, made his will, confessed his sins, admitted that the whole enterprise had been an error, and died.

The gentleman who did these things would have remained utterly obscure had he not done them; and even then he would be unknown to fame had no history of him and them been written. But one was written, and it enjoys the reputation of being perhaps the best novel in the world. Not that its author ever speaks of it as fiction. He says it is history, or if you like biography; and he does not even claim credit for its composition. He merely translated it into Spanish from the Arabic original of one Cid Hamet. He

From *Don Quixote's Profession*. © 1958 Columbia University Press.

assumes it to be true, but he made up none of its details, just as he had
nothing to do with the grand conception—either the historian's conception
of his subject or the subject's conception of himself. This last, of course,
could never have been invented by another, least of all by any novelist. No,
the truth about this gentleman is stranger than fiction can permit itself to be.
If he had not lived he would never have been imagined. He did live, though,
and here is his history.

The tale thus rescued from oblivion by Cervantes is both simple and
mysterious. The sign of its simplicity is that it can be summarized in a few
sentences. The sign of its mysteriousness is that it can be talked about
forever. It has indeed been talked about as no other story ever was. For a
strange thing happens to its readers. They do not read the same book. Or if
they do, they have different theories about it. There were never so many
theories about anything, one is tempted to say, as there are about *Don
Quixote*. Yet it survives them all, as any masterpiece must do if it would live.
A classic in the end must elude even its subtlest commentator. And so *Don
Quixote* remains truer than anything that has been said or can be said about
it. Nor is this doubted by those who know it best and love it most, though
they may have their theories too. They are the most reluctant, because of
their love, to discourse upon the essence of the book at the expense of its
being, upon its idea rather than its life. It lives, they say, and has its being in
all of the many words that make it up. They are beautiful words, and they
have their own excuse for occurring where they do. Listen to them and you
will have the life, at least the life; and after this it may turn out that nothing
else will matter.

Let us do no less than that, and certainly no more, with the beginning
of *Don Quixote*. Let us see what the words say, and let us try to have no theory
about them. Sooner or later we may fail, but at the start it should be easy.
And what do we hear Cervantes telling us? Not, for instance, that his hero
thought himself to be something or someone other than the man he was. He
suffered from no delusion as to his identity. It was merely that he had been
reading many books, and out of them he formed a conception of life as he
would henceforth live it if he could. He would live, that is to say, as knights
once did in the romances of chivalry. His error, if error it was, consisted in
taking these romances as history rather than as fiction; in believing, for
example, that Amadis of Gaul himself had ever lived in the same sense that
Julius Caesar did, or Charlemagne. Everybody in Spain read the romances,
but nobody else believed them as this gentleman believed them. They had
been written for fun, and they were to be read for fun. You finished one and
you began another, and then you finished that; but there was no change in
you except that you had been amused. But the logic of our gentleman, having

a different premise, went on to a different conclusion. The life of a knight could be lived again. It even *should* be lived again, since the world now was in as bad a way as it had been in the time of Amadis.

And still he did not think he *was* a knight. He merely thought he could become one if he took the trouble. And he took much trouble, deliberately, step by conscious step. He changed his name to Don Quixote; it had been something like that before, but the new form struck him as better. He got together a suit of armor; he gave his old horse a name, Rozinante, that seemed fitting; and he decided upon a mistress. He had no mistress, but he took one in his mind and called her Dulcinea. Nor was she wholly imaginary. A neighbor girl, Aldonza Lorenzo, had been of interest to him once, without her knowing or caring that this was so. In any case she would do, as his bony horse would do, as his great-grandfather's rusty armor would do, and as his own new name would do. He was ready now to imitate the knights of old. It is well to observe that imitation was his aim. Not impersonation, and not deception. Least of all would it be self-deception. He knew very well who he was. The only question was whether he would be able to act the part he had chosen. He was lean and strong, and so he might endure the necessary hardships. But could he think, feel, and above all talk like a knight? If he could not, then his self-education had been imperfect.

It had been good, however, in many branches of learning. He could just as well have decided to live the life of a hermit or a saint, since he was proficient in the literature of devotion; or of a scholar, since his erudition was immense; or of a shepherd, since he had read and absorbed many pastorals. Indeed his niece, when he returned home the first time and it was deemed necessary to burn the romances that she, like the barber and the curate, supposed had made him mad, insisted that the pastorals in his library should be fed to the same flames, lest in the event of his being cured of his desire to be a knight he should "turn shepherd, and so wander through the woods and fields." She knew her uncle well. Perhaps she was not aware that he had once played with the idea of writing a romance of chivalry, or at any rate of completing one that had been left without an end. This was before the idea seized him of imitating in action the heroes of all such works. And if she had known she would scarcely have objected, since writing is a quiet occupation, done at a desk. But she did surely see the intensity inside the man: an intensity that might lead only God knew where, and maybe to the woods and fields.

His decision in favor of the knightly role was determined, we may think, by the very learning it entailed. The discipline of knighthood was to him the sum of all the arts and sciences; was wisdom itself; was a liberal education. Even before he became obsessed by the romances—an obsession so extreme that he sold pieces of his land to buy more books—he must have been distinguished for his erudition. His eloquence at all times, his acuteness as a critic, his marvelous memory for details out of the remotest authors mark him as a scholar, a man of intellect and sensibility. His power to fascinate others with his conversation is never questioned, least of all by the reader of the book whose hero he is. But he is most learned in the subject of romance. It has become his specialty; it has even grown into a pedantry. No other knight was ever so deeply versed in the philosophy of the game.

Amadis of Gaul, for instance, was no scholar. He was a great gentleman: "A man of few words, slowly provoked, and quickly pacified." And his romance still deserves its fame. It is simple, clear, and exciting, not to say excellently moral. We cannot disagree with the barber and the curate when they exempt it from the burning, nor can we think it too quaint that our own gentleman insists upon its hero's having lived and moved and had his being. "I dare almost say, I have seen Amadis of Gaul with these very eyes." We may have said the same thing about Hamlet, Falstaff, Achilles, Odysseus, Squire Western, and Pickwick; and may have wondered why others protested, though we refrained from calling them mad as Don Quixote did the Canon of Toledo because the Canon refused to believe in the existence of Amadis. Amadis was both courageous and gentle; his deportment at the court of the Emperor in Constantinople is the deportment of a man so witty and sweet of tongue that he can make us think of Dulcinea's lover. And as he went by several names—Beltenebros, the Knight of the Green Sword, the Greek Knight—so Don Quixote could become in turn the Knight of the Woeful Figure and the Knight of the Lions. Yet Amadis was no scholar. For one thing, he was "a man of few words." Don Quixote is Nestor by comparison. And one could scarcely say of Don Quixote that he was "slowly provoked" or "quickly pacified." Amadis was a beautiful animal, and as such he had the temperance for which we envy beasts. He did not have to talk about being a knight because he *was* a knight. Don Quixote, being at best an imitation knight, had of course to talk like one, but then he had—or he thought he had—to talk about the importance and virtue of doing so. And of acting the part so vehemently, on a stage containing no others of his kind, that the nature of his role could never be mistaken, even though this meant that he would have to be extravagant and rash.

And now a theory about him does emerge. It is that he was first and last an actor, a skillful and conscious actor, who wrote his own play as he proceeded and of course kept the center of its stage. "In my very childhood," he said once, "I loved shows, and have been a great admirer of dramatic presentations from my youthful days." "Plays," he told Sancho, are "the resemblance of realities," and deserve to be loved because "they are all instrumental to the good of the commonwealth, and set before our eyes those looking-glasses that reflect a lively representation of human life; nothing being able to give us a more just idea of nature, and what we are or ought to be, than comedians and comedies." This can remind us of Hamlet, his contemporary, who spoke of a mirror held up to nature, who had a weakness for theatricals, who himself is the best actor in his play, and who may or may not have been mad. We shall never know what Shakespeare thought about him on the last point, and we shall never know whether Cervantes held the theory held by every other person in his book, namely that the Don was mad: had forgotten who he was, did not know what he did, was literally deluded. Upon acquaintance, to be sure, he strikes everyone as sane on every other subject than knighthood; on arms, on art, on politics, on religion, on manners, on food and sleep. But on knighthood he is cracked. And even if there are those who might grant, if the question were raised, that he is only acting like a knight, they would still think it madness to do that. In a theater, yes; but this man does it on the highways of Spain, he makes the world his stage.

And right there is the crucial question. Supposing Don Quixote to have been in his initial conception of himself an actor and nothing but an actor, did he in fact forget that this was so, did he confuse the actor with the man, the stage with life, the pretense with reality? It is something like the question we ask about Hamlet: having decided to put on an "antic disposition" in order to deceive or reassure others, did he end by becoming infected with the germ of madness thus nursed in his imagination; or, to put it another way, is there any difference finally between the madman some think him and the intense, passionate, perilously overwrought, and extremely perplexed person of genius whom anyone can recognize him as being? Either question is difficult to answer. But in Don Quixote's case it is not impossible to say that he does always know what he is doing; that he has his own reasons for what he does; and that if these would be nobody else's reasons, that is only because there is and was nobody quite like him in the world. He is that rare thing in literature, a completely created character. He is so real that we cannot be sure we understand him.

It is said of him on one occasion that he must be mad because he cannot help doing what he does. Carrasco and Cecial, who have gone after him to bring him home, and for their purpose have dressed as he is dressed, in the accouterments of knighthood, suddenly look to themselves as mad as he. Or so it seems to Cecial, though Carrasco, having been educated at Salamanca, can say: "He that only plays the fool for his fancy may give over when he pleases," whereas the Don is condemned by insanity to play the fool forever. But that very Don will give over in the end; and until then it simply does not please him to do so. When the ploughman who has rescued him from the tangle of his armor—he is on the way home, shortly after his first leaving it, to provide himself with money, clean shirts, and a squire (this will be Sancho)—when the ploughman, his near neighbor, hears him calling himself Baldwin and Abindarez, he says to him that he is only "Senior Quexada"; and Don Quixote answers him with seven famous words. "I know very well who I am." This could mean, of course, that he knows he is Baldwin or Abindarez and therefore is mad. But it could also mean just what it says. It could mean in addition: "Very well, my man, I am doing what to your poor wit may seem a crazy thing, but I have my own reason and my own method, and your part is to pick me up without further argument or ado." Whatever it means, it is worthy of being remembered throughout the long book which in a sense it introduces. Halfway through that book its hero will say in exasperation: "Heaven knows my meaning." Perhaps only heaven does.

"All I aim at," he tells the barber midway in his career, "is only to make the world sensible how much they are to blame in not laboring to revive those most happy times in which the order of knight-errantry was in its full glory." This is after the barber has been telling him of a madman who thought himself Neptune. Don Quixote, rejecting the parallel, announces his actor's, his propagandist's, aim; just as in the house of Don Diego he will implore young Don Lorenzo to consider "the vast advantages that would result" in the present age from the assistance of knights like those of old. Why shouldn't the thing be tried? He is always asking that question, even of those who doubt the actuality of knights in former ages. He is certain that they were actual, but even if they were not, the very idea of them, available now as then, is the idea that best expresses itself in the phrase "greatness of mind." Greatness of mind can exist again in those who cultivate it. His project is to cultivate a set of manners and actions that will make him look to outsiders like one who has the thing within him. The thing itself, however, is all that is ultimately important.

Seen in this aspect, Don Quixote has analogues at any time: the teacher who assumes maturity in his students and so gives them every thought he has; the gentleman whose manners consist in supposing that all other men are gentlemen too, and all women ladies; the statesman who takes it for granted that the people he rules are serious and can understand the best thing he can say; the poet who writes in the faith that his audience is no less subtle and profound, and no less wise, than himself. Such persons are often called, if not precisely mad, then foolish for believing that the best can ever be. Or be again, in a world grown cynical and degenerate. Such a world doubts its own history: its Founding Fathers, say, were never what some sanguine people think they were. Yet one who can believe in them can imitate them now; and in so doing may become a statesman, and in that capacity restore the temper of a better time.

To speak like this is to put the best face on our hero, to make the most that can be made of his madness, if mad he was. He has a worst face, too, and it is high time to speak of that. He wears it when he does violence to harmless creatures who get in his way. We wince when he assaults the sheep, exclaiming that they are armies, and kills a number of them before he can be stopped. So with the funeral at night, with its strange torches which Cervantes deliberately makes beautiful so that we shall wince the more when Don Quixote, riding against them, works havoc among the mourners, one of whom even suffers a broken leg. We do not mind so much that he risks his own skin against windmills; that is his business, amusing to us or otherwise; but we do find him painful when he hurts people who in no sense deserve it. His acting now becomes extravagant with a vengeance; his role grows ruthless; he behaves more like a lunatic than like a knight; he is fanatical, as if he thought himself, like Providence, privileged to seem cruel. He lives by his own law, and does not disarm our criticism by doing great good in the end. He does no good to the boy whom the father is whipping; indeed, he only gets him whipped further as soon as his own back is turned. He does no good by freeing the galley slaves, or by beating monks and muleteers. And while we smile at the brilliant way he takes of saying he is above law and custom, we do not forget that in so far as he acts out such a part he is a maniac on the loose. As a knight, of course, he pays no bills for lodging or food. His motto is Pistol's: "Base is the slave that pays." Nor does he think he should ever be brought before a judge. "We are exempt from courts of judicature," he informs an officer of the Holy Brotherhood whose members are devoted to the task of ridding Spain's roads of its highwaymen, and indeed all Spain of its troublemakers. To the Brotherhood Don Quixote is himself a troublemaker, whatever claims he may make for himself as one who would rid the same country of its numerous evils. Here in other words is a rivalry between the law and one who says he *is* the law; and this rivalry, in the nature of things, never comes to an end. It cannot do so as long as Don Quixote keeps his faith and maintains his role.

He maintains it with astonishing ability. Sancho, for instance, thinking at the inn to escape without paying as his master had, is caught at the gate and tossed in a blanket. Sancho cannot carry the thing off; he is worse than a poor actor, he is no actor at all. He speaks what is on his mind, in accents that are native to him. And he feels sympathy when to do so is out of order. The knight he serves rarely demeans himself by making apologies for distressful things he has done. He may not be aware that he has caused distress; but even when it is called to his attention he keeps his head high, he is too lofty to ask people's pardons. His errors—for he does commit errors— have a way of coming home to his horizon; but he has a way of not seeing them there, or if he does, of explaining them away. He would give his attention to the whipped boy except for the fact that he is busy with a knight's duties: he must save the Princess Micomicona; so it is left to Sancho to comfort the poor lad. And it is customary with him to insist that even though he has injured somebody by mistake—which is to say, has mistaken him for something other than what he is—still, it was a good mistake, an honorable mistake, since it consisted only of misinterpreting appearances, and if the appearances had been in fact the reality he supposed them he was altogether to be praised for his forthright manner of attack.

He has succeeded at any rate in becoming at home in his role. The hostess of the inn who sees him as "a man of another world" is paying him the compliment that most would please him. He really does act and talk like an old-world man, with connections running clear back to the Age of Gold which he can so handsomely apostrophize. He has the language of this age at all times on his tongue, as he has its logic. It is no less essential, he tells Vivaldo, for knights to have ladies than for skies to have stars. Heine was to say the same thing centuries later, and in the same fashion to enjoy the figure:

> For with love there must be ladies,
> And the lady was as needful
> To the tuneful minnesinger
> As, to bread and butter, butter.

Who can doubt, hearing Don Quixote in his most eloquent harangues, that he knew he was eloquent and relished eloquence as an art? No knight in any romance ever talked more perfectly about his lady than this knight talks about Dulcinea, "lovely enemy of my repose." To imitate eloquence one must somehow share its inspiration. The Don can turn off his rhetoric when he has no need for it; he can sound like Sancho when he will. But when he would sound like Amadis of Gaul he can do that too.

Nor can we doubt the relish he takes in this. He is having a good time. So good a time that he develops a rich humor in himself. Notoriously he is laughed at, but he laughs too, and by no means always at others. On a certain morning when the sun shows him that it was fulling mills, not giants, which he had heard the night before and summoned his courage to oppose, he laughs almost as heartily as Sancho does at the memory of the tall words he had cast upon the wind. Not quite as heartily, for Sancho overdoes it on his part, going even so far as to parody those words. "Am I, who am a Knight," thunders his master, "bound to know the meaning of every mechanic noise, and distinguish between sound and sound?" The question itself is delicious, and its asker knows it; just as he knows in Part II how to pull Sancho's leg by reciting the marvels he had met in the Cave of Montesinos—the marvels, mixed with such items as that he had blown his nose in the darksome cavern in order to make sure he was awake. His insistence in the Enchanted Bark that they have sailed thousands of miles is an answer to Sancho's statement that it is twenty years since they left La Mancha. His excellent relation with Sancho all along has rested upon a mutual understanding in which humor played its part. Did he expect Sancho to believe that an enchanter immobilized him so that he could do no more than gaze over the innyard wall as the squire got tossed in a blanket? Does he expect to be taken seriously when he speculates aloud that the voice under the ground—we know it is Sancho, fallen into a pit—is the voice of a soul in purgatory? So much humor, so easily and so naturally expressed, is not the mark of a madman. It is not demonic humor; it is pleasantry, it is power and wisdom at play; and probably it is what makes Sancho love him so much that he can never leave him.

No reader forgets the Don's habit, formed early in the book, of explaining awkward occurrences by saying that enchanters have been busy: they have altered people's faces, they have caused objects to appear and disappear. It is a convenient device, and one's memory may not reach back to the moment of its conception. This seems to have been the moment when Don Quixote's housekeeper, asked where his study is, says, as she has been instructed: "What study?" For while he was in bed recovering from his first sally the door to the room where he kept his books had been removed and the wall plastered over. And the niece remarks that a conjurer or enchanter must be to blame. Why may it not be supposed that Don Quixote, always, like a good actor, alert to clues, saw at once the advantage of such a dodge, and determined to use it whenever it should come in handy? If so, it must have delighted him, when he called the windmills giants, to hear Sancho say: "What giants?" The trick would last him as long as he cared to use it—of course, with variations.

He will often find himself in the presence of other persons who are acting parts, either to compete with him or to humor him into going home; or, as is sometimes the case, out of sheer roguery, for the sake of deceiving and cheating others. He will come through such competition with the highest honors; there is no actor in the book who is half as fine as he. The theatricals of Cardenio's friends are amateur by any just comparison—either, that is to say, the theatricals they habitually enact as ladies and gentlemen of fashion, or those they stage for what they suppose to be the benefit of the old madman they would hoodwink. There are many interesting ironies in the scene where Dorothea, claiming to be a damsel in distress, kneels before the mounted Knight and implores his help. One of these ironies is that she *is* distressed, as we have just learned by hearing her tell her tale of broken love; though of course we know that she is not the Princess Micomicona, in danger from a devilish giant. Another irony is there for her to measure when the Knight makes his first response. We do not know what she had expected to hear; certainly not these words that surpass in beauty the best she has ever read in any romance. Don Quixote had doubtless been represented to her by the barber and the curate as some sort of ancient fool who scarcely knows what he is babbling; but out of him comes a stream of words such as only great gentlemen can speak; and in his very manner there is "an awful grace and civility." She might well repent her decision to deceive so distinguished a person, mad or no. And here a third irony could lurk. For the Don may have labored toward just this result: her repentance, and beyond that her admiration at the skill with which he speaks his lines. How is one to know for sure that he believes her tale? It is well told, for she has read the romances and absorbed their style, and naturally he likes the way she tells it; but does he believe it? We shall never know, any more than we shall know whether the moving thanks he offers to the innkeeper's wife and her daughter and her maid when he leaves them to go home in the wooden cart are intended to strike them dumb with a sense of the injustice they have done him; or any more than we shall know, when he hangs by his hands outside the inn window, whether he wishes he had never got himself into such a pickle; or any more than we shall know in Part II whether he believes the Duke and the Duchess. More of them later; yet it is worth while to consider their castle as the best appointed stage on which he ever acts; it contains his largest and most varied audience, and is the most opulent in its costumes and its lighting.

Don Quixote is rarely alone with us so that we may see what he would be like had he not an audience. If nobody else is with him, Sancho is. Yet Sancho does leave him once in the Black Mountain, when he goes off with the letter to Dulcinea, and we are not surprised to discover a conspicuous quiet in our hero's behavior. He no longer acts the madman. Left to himself, he is controlled and serene. In his own soul he may be always self-contained. As a private individual he does have his proper secrets—for example, he is modest, and will let none of the Duchess's maids undress him. Only Sancho may do that; and when Sancho goes off to govern his island he must do it by himself. Somehow this tells us volumes concerning a sanity he spends most of his days disguising.

And all the while there is that other role of shepherd ready to be assumed. He meets many goatherds, one of whom converses with his goats; he meets the beautiful Marcella, a girl of station who finds it convenient to dress like a shepherdess and roam the mountains about her home until the day arrives when she shall know which one of her many suitors she would marry; he is regularly reminded of the pastoral romances whose lovesick heroes he could imitate if it ever struck his fancy to do so. He holds the temptation off until the end, and even then it comes to nothing. The role of shepherd is less rich than that of knight. There is less learning in it, less depth, less morality, less metaphysic. He prefers the grand role that implies all other roles. He continues acting like a knight.

Nor does this need to mean that he merely pretends. To act as he acts is more than to ape; to imitate as he does is finally to understand. What is the difference between acting like a great man and being one? To act like a poet is to write poems; to act like a statesman is to ponder the nature of goodness and justice; to act like a knight is to think and feel like one. When we tell a boy to act like a man we are not advising him to be dishonest. "Act well your part; there all the honor lies"—no one has ever detected cynicism in Pope's line. We even urge people to act natural, as if to be themselves required the exercise of art. And it does, as those unsure of themselves well know. All they have to do is to become sure; and then we shall say in praise of them that they are acting like themselves. A mysterious region, this, and Don Quixote knows it to its utmost boundaries. If he did not—if he were nothing but a pretender, which is to say a poor actor—we should not be talking of him now. We are talking of him because we suspect that in the end he did become a knight. He thought his part through. Otherwise how could he have stunned the prostrate Dorothea with such words as these? "Rise, Lady, I beseech you; I grant you the boon which your singular beauty demands." And later on, how could he have stunned her again when he replied thus to her egregious flatteries? "No more, Madam, I beseech you. Spare me the trouble of hearing myself praised, for I mortally hate whatever may look like adulation; and though your compliments may deserve a better name, my ears are too modest to be pleased with any such discourse; 'tis my study to deserve and to avoid applause. All I will venture to say is, that, whether I have any valor or not, I am wholly at your service, even at the expense of the last drop of my blood." We can assume that Don Quixote spoke these lines as if he understood them, and spoke them with a corresponding beauty. But we must also remember that he composed them on the spot. He had no script. He was actor and playwright both. He was a hero made real as only the finest art achieves reality. And this in a book whose very problem is reality, a book which calls in question the existence of knights and the sanity of an obscure man who insisted that he could be one.

The world he walked and spoke in was a wonderful copy of the world that everybody knows, the world we think of every day as real. It has been justly said that no novel is more real than *Don Quixote*, and this is true even if we consider it without its hero. Cervantes placed him where all possible light could shine on the figure he cut. We tend to forget the author as we read, but we should pause occasionally to take note of the remarkable, the daring, thing he has done. He has set a knight riding down Main Street, and of all merciless places, in Spain. It had been relatively easy for the authors of the romances to make their knights attractive. Given a willingness in their readers to find the spectacle pleasing, all they had to do was to fill the landscape with armored men who had no other occupation than that of fighting for their ladies—who, waiting in their castles, had no other need than to be beautiful and anxious day by day. Chivalry by this account was a daydream, shared in a conspiracy of pretense by author and reader alike, and the world it took place in was not required to contain such gritty essences as peasants on their mules, artisans at their lathes, traders at their desks, or thieves and beggars in the back streets of cities. It was not expected that dust or wind should be present, or money, or charity, or filth, or such kinds of food as crusts of bread, lumps of cheese, and slices of raw onion. And the result even then was a charming literature, as Cervantes knows as well as his hero, and as well as every other person in the story. Even the hardheaded housekeeper, at home in La Mancha, wants to sprinkle her master's books with holy water to exorcise the sorcery in them. Yet it had not been a real literature as Cervantes, starting to write his masterpiece, comprehended the term. Into this masterpiece he would put everything he knew, all that he smelled as well as all that he thought and imagined.

And upon every item of his account he bestowed the dignity of an incomparable style. The stream of his words is beautiful and strong, nor does it object to any article it is called upon to float toward its natural destination. All things, all persons, ride the current of this world as if they had a right to do so. Cervantes once calls the work he pretends to be translating a "grave, high-sounding, minute, soft, and humorous history." Grave and humorous: it is comedy at its best, with everything remembered out of life, and with all things in it weighted equally, justly. And because of that equal and just weight, nothing feels heavier than it should, neither the fine knight on Rozinante nor the plain people who stare at him and doubt that he is as fine as he says he is. There is a lightness in the book that makes every reader love it as he loves his own mind. It is both vast and delicate, both formidable and buoyant. The writer of it—we can never doubt this—was happy as he wrote.

He must have been happiest when his hero, come home to provide himself with a squire, thought of his neighbor Sancho and persuaded him to go along. There has never been a better device for fiction than this of two men who see the same things but consider them differently. And so just is Cervantes, so equal in his love, that neither of them is ever at a disadvantage in our view. Each is a created individual, with a world of his own which the other must accept—not approve, but certainly accept, as if it had as much right to exist and be believed in as his own. Each calls the other names; each accuses the other of being mad; they quarrel, they fall out and are silent for long stretches; they insist they do not understand each other. Yet their mutual love increases until at last they are, as others say, one man.

"Do you know where you are?" cries Don Quixote in the castle of the Duke when Sancho has disturbed decorum by insisting that Dapple, his ass, be suitably stabled and fed. "Every man," says Sancho, "must tell his wants, be he where he will. Here I bethought myself of Dapple, and here I spoke of him. Had I called him to mind in the stable, I would have spoken of him there." He has only one language, the language of the Panzas, and he uses it as language was intended to be used, to make known the thought within. Don Quixote is master of many languages, just as he is master of many thoughts, and he inhabits as it were a variety of worlds, though all of them may be one world, his world, in the end. But Sancho inhabits *this* world and no other; and he inhabits it so simply that he becomes, both for Cervantes and for us who are looking on, its perfect symbol. Don Quixote does not merely ride through this world; he takes it with him, he looks at it and listens to it every day, he sleeps and feeds with it, he argues with it, he fights with it and makes up, he accepts it always as being there. Nor does it ever change. Stubbornly, it is what it is, as he is too. The Don and the Squire never convince each other, even though they take a greater and greater pleasure in adventuring side by side.

Each of them, too, has a household out of which he comes; the reality of both is documented. Don Quixote has no wife and children, but we shall never forget his niece, his housekeeper, and his neighbors, for they go with him even though he thinks he has left them behind; unique as he is among them, he still cannot be separated from them any more than the heart can be removed from the body, or the sting from the bee. Sancho Panza has of course his own family, nor does he ever want to forget the wife and daughter he has been persuaded to abandon. They are not really abandoned. They are constantly, and sometimes guiltily, in his thoughts. The sense of guilt is not perhaps complete in Sancho; if it were, he would make good his frequent threats of going home. It is often no more than an excuse for blaming his master. "See," says the squire, "how you plucked me out of the bosom of my family, and all for this"—a tossing in a blanket, a beating by a rogue. Yet he does miss his little house and the people in it who are so much like him. Twice they rejoice to see him coming home over the hill outside the village, and twice he rejoices with them. And when he is governing his island nothing gives him more satisfaction than such a letter as this from Teresa his wife, with news in it of Sanchica his daughter:

"The news here is, that Berrueca has married her daughter to a sorry painter that came hither, pretending to paint anything. The township set him to paint the King's arms over the Town Hall. He asked 'em two ducats for the job, which they paid him. So he fell to work, and was eight days a-daubing, but could make nothing of it at last; and said he could not hit upon such piddling kind of work, and so gave 'em their money again. . . . Pedro de Lobo's son has taken orders, and shaved his crown, meaning to be a priest. Minguilla, Mingo Silvato's grand-daughter, heard of it, and sues him upon a promise of marriage; ill tongues do not stick to say she has been with child by him, but he stiffly denies it. We have no olives this year, nor is there a drop of vinegar to be got for love or money. A company of soldiers went through this place, and carried along with them three wenches out of the town. I don't tell thee their names, for mayhaps they will come back, and there will not want some that will marry 'em, for better for worse. Sanchica makes bone-lace, and gets her three half-pence a day clear, which she saves in a box with a slit, to go towards buying household stuff. The fountain in the market is dried up. A thunderbolt lately fell upon the pillory—there may they all light. I expect thy answer to this. Heaven send thee long to live, longer than myself, or rather, as long; for I would not willingly leave thee behind me in this world. Thy wife, Teresa Panza."

The reality of this is not the only reality in *Don Quixote*, but it is perhaps the basic one; it is the ground on which all other realities stand. And it is firm ground, built there by hands that know of what minerals the earth was originally composed. Nor is it laid down with condescension or disgust. Cervantes respects the world his people walk on, however high or low they hold their heads. Not the least of his triumphs is that he manages neither to satirize nor to idealize his so-called common people. They seem to be exactly what they ought to be: the people of this world, for better or for worse, with no doubt in their heads that they should exist and respect themselves. Merely to hear them talking makes one happier, more reassured, than one knows how to say. As when, for a final instance, the innkeeper's wife and daughter are attending to Don Quixote's bruises. The bruises were inflicted by cudgels, but Sancho, to save his master's dignity, not to speak of his own, since he was cudgeled too, has told the women they were the result of a fall from the top of a high rock. "And by the way," says he, "I beseech you save a little of that same tow and ointment for me too, for I don't know what's the matter with my back, but I fancy I stand mainly in want of a little greasing too." "What, I suppose you fell too," says the landlady. "Not I," says Sancho, "but the very fright that I took to see my master tumble down the rock has so wrought upon my body that I'm as sore as if I had been sadly mauled." "It may well be as you say," puts in the daughter; "for I have dreamed several times that I have been falling from the top of a high tower without ever coming to the ground; and when I have waked, I have found myself as out of order, and as bruised, as if I had fallen in good earnest." Meanwhile Maritornes, the entirely illiterate maid of the inn, has been holding a candle so that her mistress could see the Don. "How do you call this same gentleman?" she asks the squire. "He's Don Quixote de la Mancha," replies Sancho, "and he is a knight-errant, and one of the primest and stoutest that ever the sun shined on." "A knight-errant," cries the wench. "Pray, what's that?"

HARRY LEVIN

The Example of Cervantes

To crown him with an adjective of his own choosing, Cervantes continues to be the exemplary novelist. It is a truism, of course, that he set the example for all other novelists to follow. The paradox is that, by exemplifying the effects of fantasy on the mind, he pointed the one way for fiction to attain the effect of truth. We state his achievement somewhat more concretely when we say that he created a new form by criticizing the old forms. *Don Quixote*, in terms of its intention and impact, constituted an overt act of criticism. Through its many varieties of two-sided observation, there runs a single pattern: the pattern of art embarrassed by confrontation with nature. This is the substance of the critical comment that every chapter makes in a differing context. We can test it by considering the implications of two such passages, taken from familiar and typical episodes, widely separated yet closely related. (With some cross-reference to the original Spanish in the interests of semantics, and a good deal of paraphrase in the interests of condensation, I shall be quoting Cervantes from the contemporaneous English translation of Thomas Shelton. Spelling will be modernized, and parenthetical numbers will refer to any standard text.)

Our first passage occurs in Chapter XXII of the First Part, which is entitled "Of the liberty Don Quixote gave to many wretches, who were a-carrying perforce to a place they desired not." Let us pause for a moment

---

From *Contexts of Criticism*. © 1957 by the President and Fellows of Harvard College.

over this heading. It turns into a characteristically dry understatement as soon as we realize that "the place they desired not" was the galleys. But the emphasis falls on the two common nouns in the main clause, "liberty" and "wretches." *Libertad!* The very word, which was to reverberate with such easy sonority for Walt Whitman, carried a poignant overtone for Cervantes. After the famous battle of Lepanto in which he lost the use of his hand, as he never tires of retelling, he had been captured by pirates and sold as a slave, and had perforce spent five long years in Algerian captivity. That enslavement, in a place Cervantes desired not, must have lent special meaning to Don Quixote's gesture of liberation. The tale later told by the Captive—the Spanish Captain enslaved at Algiers who recovers his greatest joy, lost liberty—is highly romanticized; but it hints that the actual truth was stranger than the incidental fiction when it mentions a certain Cervantes ("*tal de Saavedra*") and the deeds he did—and all to achieve liberty ("*y todas por alcanzar libertad,*" I, xl).

Hence the wretches are more to be pitied than scorned; and here the key word, *desdichados,* is not so much a term of contempt as an ironic expression of fellow feeling. It may not be irrelevant to recall that *El Desdichado* is also the title Gérard de Nerval gives to his melancholy sonnet on the romantic hero. A similar ambiguity characterizes the French *les misérables* or the Russian *neschastniki.* The undertones of humanitarian sympathy, implied when Don Quixote liberates the convicts, come to the surface when he finally reaches Barcelona, and we are brought face to face with galley slaves. Again we cannot help thinking of the author—not because his book is, in any sense, autobiographical; but because it is, like most great books, the unique distillation of mature experience. Behind the book stands a soldier of misfortune who had encountered many setbacks on his personal journey to Parnassus. Having tried his one good hand at virtually all the flowery forms of the artificial literature of that baroque period, he had addressed himself to the hazards of the road in the uncongenial guise of tax collector. And again it is of himself that he speaks with rueful humor, when the Priest and the Barber hold their inquisition over the books in Don Quixote's library. Among those which are set aside from the burning is the pastoral romance of *Galatea* by Miguel de Cervantes Saavedra. The Priest mitigates his criticism with a pun: this author is "*más versado en desdichas que en versos*"—better versed in misfortunes than in verses (I, vi).

Don Quixote's ideal of humanistic perfection is to be equally well versed in arms and letters. It might be opined that he fails because his military training has lagged so far behind his literary preparation. Something like the contrary might be maintained about his creator. At all events, after all he had been through, Cervantes would have been the very last man to cherish romantic illusions on the subject of adventure. He was therefore just the man to dramatize a distinction which has since become an axiom, which has indeed become so axiomatic that it might well be called Cervantes' formula. This is nothing more nor less than a recognition of the difference between verses and reverses, between words and deeds, *palabras* and *hechos*— in short, between literary artifice and that real thing which is life itself. But literary artifice is the only means that a writer has at his disposal. How else can he convey his impression of life? Precisely by discrediting those means, by repudiating that air of bookishness in which any book is inevitably wrapped. When Pascal observed that true eloquence makes fun of eloquence, he succinctly formulated the principle that could look to Cervantes as its recent and striking exemplar. It remained for La Rochefoucauld to restate the other side of the paradox: some people would never have loved if they had not heard of love.

The chapter that sees the convicts liberated is rather exceptional in its direct approach to reality. The preceding chapter has been a more devious and characteristic excursion into the domain of romance. Its theme, which has come to be a byword for the transmuting power of imagination, as well as for Don Quixote's peculiar habit of imposing his obsession upon the world, is the barber's basin he takes for the fabulous helmet of Mambrino, stolen from Rianldo by Sacripante in the *Orlando Furioso*. If the recovery of this knightly symbol is effected without undue incident, it is because the barber has no wish to fight; subsequently, when he returns to claim his property, he allows himself to be persuaded that it is really a helmet which has been enchanted to look like a basin. Such is the enchantment Don Quixote invokes to rationalize his defeats and embarrassments. Delusions of grandeur, conveniently enough, are sustained by phobias of persecution; somehow hostile enchanters always manage to get between him and the fulfillment of his ideals. Cervantes borrowed his plot from an interlude about a peasant bemused by popular ballads; and though that *donnée* is elaborated through an infinite series of variations, it remains almost repetitiously simple. Each episode is a kind of skit in which the protagonist, attempting to put his heroic ideals into action, is discomfited by realities in the shape of slapstick comedy.

Thus deeds, with a vengeance, comment on words; and Cervantes' formula is demonstrated again and again. Afterward there are more words, pleasant discussions, "*graciosos razonamientos*"—which naturally require the presence of an amusing companion, an interlocutor, a *gracioso*. The hero of cape-and-sword drama is squired by such a buffoon; the courtier is often burlesqued by the zany who serves him; Don Quixote's servant—like Figaro or Jeeves—is cleverer, in some vital respects, than his master. Much, possibly too much, has already been written on the dualism of Don Quixote and Sancho Panza as a symbolic representation of soul and body, past and present, poetry and prose, the inner dilemmas of psychology, or the all-embracing antitheses of metaphysics. We need only remind ourselves in passing that, within this eternal comedy team, Sancho Panza's role is to assert a sense of reality. The incident of the windmills provides him with his usual cue and his classical response. When the knight beholds these machines in the distance, and asks the squire whether he too does not behold these monstrous giants, it is Sancho's function to reply with another question: "What giants?" In his person the challenging voice of empiricism does it best and its worst to refute the aprioristic frame of mind, which has since become so closely identified with the Don that we sometimes term it *Quixotry*.

Now, on the comic stage, Sancho would have the final word. In the pictorial vision of Daumier, the pair coexist within the same frame of reference as the bourgeoisie and the caricatured intellectuals. Yet in a book, where words are the only medium, Don Quixote enjoys a decided advantage; the very weakness of his position in life lends strength, as it were, to his position in literature; in the field of action he may encounter discomfiture, but in the verbal sphere he soon resumes his imaginary career. When Sancho is skeptical about the basin and goes on to doubt the rewards of knighthood, the Don simply lapses into his autistic fantasies of wish-fulfillment; and his conversation during the next few pages spins out another romance in miniature. The most elaborate of the many little romances that run through his head and through the novel figures in his argument with the Canon of Toledo at the end of the First Part, and offers Cervantes occasion to develop his theory of the comic epic in prose. The Canon, on his side, is a more erudite humanist than Sancho Panza; but he casts the weight of his learning in favor of what the critics have labeled "probability"; and he pertinently distinguishes between fictitious and truthful histories (*historia imaginada, historia verdadera*).

Don Quixote's answer is a powerful statement of the appeal of romance. Freud would have diagnosed it as the purest indulgence in the pleasure-principle, the sheerest escape from the reality-principle. It is the daydream of a golden world of gardens and castles where art improves upon nature, where blandishing damsels await the errant adventurer and every misadventure leads toward a happy ending. It is a heady and concentrated restatement of the ever-appealing myth that, in Cervantes' day, incarnated its bland archetype in Amadís of Gaul. Amadís, like every true cavalier, was by definition a paragon who surpassed all other cavaliers; his invulnerable prowess was as unparalleled as the peerless beauty of his lady, Oriana, or the perfect faithfulness of his squire, Gandalín. He was predestined to triumph over an all but endless sequence of rivals and obstacles, and to be united with his heroine in an enchanted chamber which only the bravest and fairest could enter, somewhere out of this world on an uncharted island misleadingly named Terra Firma. Meanwhile the chronicle of his adventures and those of his progeny, prolonged through five generations and twenty-four volumes, furnished the primary source of inspiration for Don Quixote, whose pattern of behavior is—to speak it profanely—a kind of *imitatio Amadís*.

Imitation is the test that Cervantes proposes, knowing full well that when nature imitates art, art reveals its innate artificiality. Literally his hero reënacts episodes from the life-cycle of his own hero, as when he assumes the name of Beltenebros and undergoes penance in the Sierra Morena. But since he aspires to combine the virtues of other heroes—the Nine Worthies, the Twelve Paladins, the aggregate muster-roll of knight errantry—he must likewise emulate Ariosto's Orlando. And since Orlando went mad for love of the fair Angelica, Don Quixote must rage in order to prove his devotion to the fair Dulcinea del Toboso. The place-name he attaches to his kitchen-maid heroine is less artistocratic than anticlimactic, particularly when it is left to dangle as the refrain of one of the poems addressed to her. The process of emulation, dedicated to a whole set of models at once, going through their motions so pedantically and overstating their claims so fanatically, tends to reduce them all to absurdity. Because this tendency is deliberate, the prevailing method is that of parody: a marvelous gift, according to Ben Jonson, which makes a work "absurder than it was." But *Amadís de Gaula* could hardly have been absurder than it was; its innumerable sequels might almost have been parodies; while *Don Quixote* might be no more than another sequel, if it had no objective vantage-point from which to chart the deviations of its subjective course.

Its protagonist sallies forth at the outset, talking to himself—as will be his wont—about the historian who will have the honor of recording the exploits he is about to accomplish (I, ii). With a dizzying shift of the time-sense, he looks back from the future upon events which have yet to take place. From first to last the narration is colored by his own self-consciousness. A much later sally is introduced by this mock-heroic sentence:

> Scarce had the silver morn given bright Phoebus leave with ardor
> of his burning rays to dry the liquid pearls on his golden locks,
> when Don Quixote, shaking off sloth from his drowsy members,
> rose up and called Sancho his squire, that still lay snorting (II, xx).

Here, with the calculated anticlimax of the last word, all the mythological ornamentation sinks into bathos. Actuality, suddenly intervening, restores our perspective to a more firmly grounded base of observation. The high-flown monologue becomes a pedestrian dialogue, which in turn restates the dialectical issue of the book. Sancho Panza, the principle dialectician, is quite aware of that variance which makes his fall into a mere hole so utterly different from Don Quixote's exploration of the Cave of Montesinos: "There saw he goodly and pleasant visions and here, I believe, I shall see nothing but snakes and toads (II, lv)." The pleasant visions are abstract and remote: the snakes and toads are concrete and immediate; the variance is all in the point of view.

The psychological contrast is reflected in the stylistic texture from the opening page, where the first paragraph is straight factual exposition, while the second echoes two florid sentences from Don Quixote's reading. Diction shows the increasing influence of Sancho's viewpoint when—amid bouquets of poetic conceit and parades of learned authority, the regular mental context of Don Quixote—Cervantes apologizes for using the homely substantive *puercos*, and thereby calling a pig a pig. Once this sort of interplay has been established, Don Quixote himself can take the metaphorical step from the sublime to the ridiculous. When Sancho reports that Dulcinea's visage is slightly blemished by a mole, he can respond with an inappropriate amplification—"Though she had a hundred moles as well as that one thou sawest in her, they were not moles but moons and bright stars"—a pretty picture which outdoes even Shakespeare's hyperbolic gibes against the Petrarchan sonneteers (II, x). The gravity of his demeanor is matched by the grandiosity of his rhetoric, a manner of speaking broadly connoted by the rhetorical term *prospopeya*. His dead-pan humor would not be humorous were some one else not there to see the joke, to watch the imitation becoming a parody by failing to meet the challenge at hand. As his purple passages are juxtaposed with Sancho's vernacular proverbs, the bookish and sluggish flow of his consciousness is freshened and quickened; flat assertion is rounded out, and soliloquy is colloquialized.

Cervantes, whose *Colloquy of the Dogs* we must not forget, was well schooled in those mixed modes of Erasmus and Lucian which—linking the early modern spirit to the late Greco-Roman—seem to express the self-questionings of a traditional culture during an epoch of rapid and far-reaching change. The literature of the Renaissance, which moves from one extreme to the other so readily, is the register of a violent effort to catch up with the expanding conditions of life. With its realization that certain themes are still untreated goes the feeling that certain techniques are becoming outmoded. The needed renewal and the strategic enlargement begin by adapting, experimenting, cross-fertilizing, and incidentally producing giants and dwarfs whose incongruous qualities merely bear witness to the overplus of creativity.

Extraordinary combinations of language, such as macaronics, waver between Latinity and the vulgar tongues. Poetry, evoking the legendary past, varies its tone from nostalgia to facetiousness. Prose impinges, entirely unaware of its hybrid possibilities as an imaginative medium. A transitional sense of disproportion makes itself felt, not only in mannerist painting, but in complementary literary genres: mock-epic, which magnifies vulgarity, applying the grand manner to commonplace matters; and travesty, which minimizes greatness, reclothing noble figures in base attire.

It will easily be seen, from page to page, how Cervantes ranges between these two reductive extremes. One of his own descriptions of his style, at the beginning of the chapter before us, oscillates from high-sounding ("*altisonante*") to trivial ("*mínima*"). This oscillation puzzled Shelton so much that he translated the latter word by one more congruent to the former: "divine" (*divina*). However, Cervantes encompasses many such disparities, bridging the gap between style and subject by the continual play of his irony. Rabelais could revel in the *mélange des genres*, parodying the quest for the Holy Grail in the cult of the Holy Bottle. A lesser writer, Robert Greene, could live between two worlds and keep them apart: first-hand journalistic accounts of the London underworld and mannered pastoral romances set in some escapist Arcadia, with very little intermixture of styles. The immeasurable contribution of Cervantes was to broaden the province of prose fiction by bringing both realms together, not in a synthesis perhaps, but in the most durable antithesis that literature has known; by opening a colloquy between the romance and the picaresque, so to speak, between *Amadís de Gaula* and *Lazarillo de Tormes*. Spain, with its strongly marked chiaroscuro of contrasts, social as well as cultural, presented the pertinent matter of fact along with the far-fetched matter of fiction. The first-person narrative of the little beggar, Lazarillo, whose harsh masters taught him to cheat or be cheated, gave Cervantes the fructifying example for an exemplary novel to which *Don Quixote* refers, *Rinconete and Cortadillo*—a tale endearing to American readers as a Sevillian adumbration of *Tom Sawyer* and *Huckleberry Finn*.

II

Having proceeded discursively, after the fashion of Rocinante, we have come back to our starting point and are ready to set out once again. Our preliminary amble has not been wasted if it has confirmed our awareness of the "disorderly order" that regulates the imaginary gardens of Cervantes, and that may emerge from the passage to which we now return. After the

gang of unfortunates bound for the galleys is released through the
officiousness of Don Quixote, he is confounded by reality in the shifty
person of their ringleader: a rogue indeed, the authentic picaroon, Ginés de
Pasamonte. Ginés, among his other dubious traits, harbors pretensions as a
man of letters; to beguile the time in prison, he declares, he has made a book
out of the story of his life. This may strengthen the bonds of affinity that
connect the present chapter with the life of Cervantes; for we know that the
author was imprisoned, through some bureaucratic complication, during the
period when he was writing *Don Quixote*; and he may be referring to that
circumstance, with his genius for rising above a situation, when his prologue
alludes to "some dark and noisome prison." In any case, Don Quixote is
curious about this particular product of incarcerated endeavors.

> "Is it so good a work?" said Don Quixote.
> "It is so good," replied Ginés, "that it quite puts down
> *Lazarillo de Tormes* and as many others as are written or shall
> write of that kind: for that which I dare affirm to you is that it
> treats of true accidents, and those so delightful that no like
> invention can be compared to them."
> "And how is the book entitled?" quoth Don Quixote.
> "It is called," said he, "*The Life of Ginés of Pasamonte*."
> "And is it yet ended?" said the knight.
> "How can it be finished," replied he, "my life being not yet
> ended?"

To mention a work of fiction in the course of another work of fiction
can be a two-edged device. It can show up the book that is mentioned,
thereby sharpening the realism of the book that does the mentioning. This
is what Ginés does for his own work at the expense of Lazarillo, and what
Cervantes is doing for *Don Quixote* at the expense of *Amadís de Gaula*,
expressly invoked by his own commendatory verses. Conversely, the
invidious comparison can glance in the other direction, as in the case of many
a derivative academic novel today: the pale reflection of a dream of the
shadow of Henry James. But that is unmitigated imitation, and it produces a
conventional literature, circumscribing novelists to the point where even
their titles must be quotations from other books. The method of Cervantes
utilized literary means to break through literary conventions and, in the very
process, invented a form substantial and flexible enough to set forth the
vicissitudes of modern society. Parody, explicitly criticizing a mode of
literature, developed into satire, implicitly criticizing a way of life.
Developing out of the debris of feudalism, the novel has waxed and waned

with the middle class. Yet in the twentieth century, according to Thomas Mann's contemporary Faust, the arts tend more than ever to parody themselves. The writer's problem, as André Gide has rephrased Cervantes' formula, is still the rivalry between the real world and the representation we make of it.

It is significant that Gide's most serious novel, which likewise probes the theme of how novels come to be written, is called *The Counterfeiters;* and that Mann's last fragment—begun forty years before and completed only, in the peculiar sense of Ginés, by the author's death—is a reversion to the picaresque cycle, *Confessions of Felix Krull.* For trickery is inherent, as artists recognize, in their business of dealing with illusion. We do well then to scrutinize some of their tricks rather closely; and Cervantes is well justified in conveying this caveat, or insight, through the mouth of an incorrigible charlatan. After all, no one can express what is by nature inexpressible. Life itself is infinitely larger than any artistic medium. However, by revealing the limitations of their medium, writers like Cervantes heighten our consciousness of what existence means. The real story of Ginés de Pasamonte, comparatively more real than the imagined *Life of Lazarillo de Tormes*, is bound to be incomplete because life is endless. It lasts forever, as Tolstoy's peasant says just before he dies in *War and Peace.* In all sincerity, therefore, we cannot say *finis*; we can only write "to be continued." And so with Cervantes, like Ginés writing in prison, and breaking off his First Part with a provisory ending and a cautionary moral: Beware of fiction! It is fictitious; that is to say, it is false. Don't let it mislead you!

The ironic consequence of his warning was the creation of an archetype, a fictional personage destined to be far more influential than Amadís of Gaul. The remarkable success of the First Part was the precondition of the Second, which is consequently more deliberate in its artistry. By that time, the latter volume announces, the fame of its predecessor has spread so widely that any lean horse would be hailed as Rocinante. The earlier conclusion, in which so little was concluded, clearly invited some continuation. Before Cervantes could take up his own tale again, the interloper who signed himself "Avellaneda" brought out his notorious sequel: an imitation of a parody. Because the impersonation had to be imitative, it could not be organic; it could not live and grow as Cervantes' original would do in his Second Part. The mysterious Avellaneda, when Cervantes finally caught up with him, all but took the place of Amadís as a satirical target, and as a measure of the distance between echoed phrases and lived experiences. Adding insult to injury, he had not only plagiarized; he had also criticized his victim for not keeping his own brain-children in character, and—even more significantly—for introducing Ginés. That scoundrel had shown a comparable ingratitude when he rewarded his liberator with a shower of stones, absconding with Don Quixote's sword and—temporarily—Sancho Panza's ass. But the Second Part arranges a further encounter and, for the knight, an opportune revenge.

This involves our second illustration, a rather more extended example which need not be cited at length, since it figures so prominently in the celebrated episode of Master Peter's puppet-show. Poetic drama—another genre which Cervantes had practiced with indifferent results—is here reduced to its most elementary level, just as prose fiction was in the instance we have been discussing. The link between these two passages, as we learn from the next chapter, is Maese Pedro himself, who turns out to be none other than Don Quixote's old enemy, Ginés. Always the escape-artist, he is now an itinerant showman, and more of a dealer in deception than ever. One of his other exhibits happens to be a fortune-telling ape, whose roguish trick is subsequently exposed. Now Cervantes was obviously fond of animals; a dog-lover and a master of the beast-fable, he satirizes war in a parable about braying asses and courtly love in a serenade of cats; the dramatis personae of his book include a traveling menagerie; but the ape, above all, is the parodistic animal. When the lovelorn Dorothea joins the friendly conspiracy to bring the knight to his senses, she poses as the Infanta Micomica of Micomicón ("Princess Monkey-Monkey of Monkeyland"). Actually a damsel in distress, she acts the part of a damsel in distress; and the make-believe story she recounts to Don Quixote is the parody of a parody, her own story.

This monkey-business, if it may be so designated, accelerates to its climax through a sequence of scenes at the inn. There the incidental stories accumulate, and there the actual personages who tell or figure in them are interrelated through the fiat of romantic coincidence. Viktor Shklovsky has aptly described this meeting-place as "a literary inn," though another emphasis would interpret it as a social microcosm. On the one hand, the relationship between letters and arms is the appropriate topic of Don Quixote's discourse; on the other, the crude farce of the wineskins and the stern intervention of the Holy Brotherhood, searching for the importunate busybody who freed the convicts, underline the romance with a touch of reality. The central interpolation is a tale which comes out of the same bag of manuscripts as some of Cervantes' *Exemplary Novels*—or so the literary host very plausibly informs his guests. It is the tale of the so-called Curious Impertinent, an almost Proustian study in point of view, wherein Anselmo's universal suspicion functions as a sort of mirror-opposite for Don Quixote's ubiquitous credulity. Characterization of the protagonist gains in depth as he passes through the levels of the characters who surround him, in their assumed roles, with their recounted adventures—sometimes tales within tales. As in Chaucer's *Canterbury Tales*, the story-tellers take on an extra dimension against the formal backdrop of their stories.

Part I situates these episodes, within the tradition of the frame-story, at an extra remove from the reader. In Part II, as the narrator proudly explains, they are unified by the divagations of a single plot. Where the First Part centered upon an inn, which the hero insisted on taking for a castle, the Second Part leads to a long sojourn at a genuine castle, where the conversation is less inspired and the horseplay heavier than at any other juncture of the book. Castles in Spain, for non-Spaniards, have proverbially symbolized the veritable fabric of romance. "Castle-building," in the library at Waverly Honour, was the state of mind that engendered the latter-day romances of Sir Walter Scott. The terrain of Don Quixote, the arid region of La Mancha, overlaps Castile, which is quite literally the land of castles. But Cervantes' castle seems to mark an anticlimactic turning point, a release from mental imprisonment, the beginning of an undeception for the knight; while it bewitches the squire, offering him a brief chance to go his own way and to impose the rough justice of the common man on the neighboring dependency of Barataria. Overshadowed by that glimpse of a democratic community, or the disillusioning city of Barcelona just ahead, chivalric entertainment may well pall. Not that the Duke and Duchess have spared any courtesy; they have humored their fantastic guest with such labored vivacity that they are accused of being madder than he; there has been more manipulation and masquerading, more play-acting and practical joking, at the castle than at the inn.

The effectiveness of the play-within-the-play lies in making the main drama more convincing: when the King interrupts the Players in *Hamlet*, we feel that at last we have come to grips with reality. One way of attaining this effect is to make the theatrical figures unconvincing; and when these are puppets rather than actors, wooden dolls imitating human beings, everything undergoes a reduction of scale; their performance becomes a mode of ridicule, as Bergson has suggested in his essay on laughter. Hence, among the many stratagems that Cervantes employs against the romance, none is more sharply conceived nor more skillfully executed then the puppet-play. His description of it commences in epic style, with the spectators—Tyrians and Trojans—falling silent, and the youthful reciter appealing to the authority of old French chronicles and Spanish ballads (II, xxvi). The setting is a city whose ancient name, Sansueña, suffuses a dreamy atmosphere. The plot concerns the Princess Melisendra, imprisoned by the Moors even as Cervantes himself has been, and her knightly rescuer, Gaiferos, who must accomplish his task by fighting the Moors as Cervantes has done—but with a difference, that crucial difference between fantasy and actuality which it is his constant purpose to emphasize.

For once Don Quixote has no need to superimpose his fancies; he need only take the presentation literally. As a matter of fact, he starts by criticizing certain details of Moorish local color. Gradually he suspends his disbelief—which has never been too strong—and enters into the spirit of the occasion so actively that, before the others can stop him, he has begun "to rain strokes upon the puppetish Moorism." The puppeteer, Ginés, alias Pedro, cries: "Hold, Señor Don Quixote, hold! and know that these you hurl down, destroy, and kill, are not real Moors but shapes made of pasteboard." And reality is restored no less abruptly than it is when Alice cries out to the creatures of Wonderland: "You're nothing but a pack of cards!" Pedro-Ginés, the arch-manipulator, the ever versatile illusionist, laments his loss for an operatic moment or two, and then shrewdly reckons it up: so much for Charlemagne split down the middle, so much for Melisendra without a nose, and so on down to the last marivedí, paid in full by Don Quixote in coin of the realm. Such mercenary language contrasts with another aspect of the show: the puppets were knocked down, we are told, "in less than two credos." This is rather a figure of speech than an article of belief; and the wax candles probably have no ritual significance; yet it is worth remembering that the word *retablo*, applied to the puppet-show, signifies primarily an altarpiece. I do not want to place undue stress on symbols which prove so brittle; but we cannot altogether ignore the iconoclasm of Cervantes, since the Inquisition did not.

In the next chapter, when the narrator swears to his own veracity as a Catholic Christian, the author himself feels obliged to point out that this protestation comes from an unbelieving Moor (II, xxvii). Elsewhere he repeatedly warns us that Moors are not to be trusted: they are "cheaters, impostors, and chemists" (II, iii). Cervantes' fictional narrator is one of these elusive infidels: an "Arabical and Manchegan historiographer" named the Cide Hamete Benengeli, who does not appear in the opening pages of the book. Don Quixote completes his first sally, saunters forth again, challenges the Biscayan, and is left sword in air by the break between the seventh and eighth chapters. In a digression, Cervantes tells us that his documentation has run out, and that we might well have been left in suspense forever; again, as in the later colloquy between Don Quixote and Ginés, life is conceived as an unfinished book. Happily, in a bazaar at Toledo, Cervantes has chanced upon an Arabic manuscript which will supply the rest of the story; and from now on the Cide Hamete will be responsible for it, even as Captain Clutterbuck or Jedediah Cleishbotham would be responsible for Scott's narrations, and other pseudonymous narrators for Stendhal's and Manzoni's. Since the author presents himself as editor, assuming the intervention of a

Spanish translator from the Arabic, the text stands at three removes from ourselves, enriched with afterthoughts like a palimpsest. This procedure has the advantages of enabling the author to digress more freely, to blame his source for indiscreet remarks, and to cultivate an air of authenticity.

But authenticity is deeply called into question on one problematic occasion, when the whole trend of the book is reversed, turning back from pragmatic demonstration to metaphysical speculation, or—in the more incisive phrase of Américo Castro—from a critique of fiction to a critique of reality. Can men's lives be so sharply differentiated from their dreams, when all is said and done? Can we live without illusion? we are asked. Don Quixote may be right, the rest of us wrong. Many of the philosophers, most of the poets, would take his side. Spanish imagination is not unique in having been fascinated by Calderón's refrain: *La vida es sueño*, life is a dream. Even Shakespeare conceded the possibility: "We are such stuff/As dreams are made on . . ." Who are we, in that event, to look down upon puppets imprisoned within the dream-city of Sansueña? May it not be that the images of ourselves created by writers, as Pirandello would urge, are more real than we are? For example, *Don Quixote*. The chapter that explores such ultimate doubts is admittedly apocryphal; it may be an intermixture of truth and falsehood, as pantomimed by Maese Pedro's ape. We are tempted to believe that Don Quixote's descent into the Cave of Montesinos is a return to the deep well of the past, the unconscious memory of the race, and that the mythical heroes sleeping there personify the ideals he struggled to practice, the ideology of the Golden Age. Yet the simple and brutal alternative persists that he may have been caught in a lie and have become a party to the general imposture.

In the absence of other witnesses, certainty continues to elude us. The best advice Don Quixote can report is the gambler's maxim spoken, curiously enough, by the flower and mirror of chivalry, Durandarte: *Paciencia y barajar*, patience and shuffle, go on with the game (II, xxiii). After the underground interview with the dead heroes, the next stage is the fable about the asses, and then the puppetry of Pedro-Ginés; and each successive chapter is a station on the pilgrimage of disenchantment. Disarmed, dismounted, and finally discomfited, the former knight is on his way homeward, when the sight of shepherds rouses his flagging impulses to their last wish-dream. Sancho, of course, has an important part in it:

> I'll buy sheep and all things fit for our pastoral vocation; and calling myself by the name of shepherd Quixotiz and thou the shepherd Pansino, we will walk up and down the hills, through woods and meadows, singing and versifying and drinking the

liquid crystal of the fountains, sometimes out of the clear springs
and then out of the swift-running rivers . . . (II, lxvii).

But Don Quixote has come to the end of his life and, accordingly, of his
book. It remained for other books to parody the pastoral romances, as his
had parodied the romances of chivalry: notably a French disciple of
Cervantes, Charles Sorel, who wrote a novel entitled *Anti-Romance*, and
subtitled *The Wayward Shepherd* (*L'Anti-roman, ou le berger extravagant*). That
would be another story; but perhaps the term *anti-romance* might be usefully
borrowed to generalize a major premise of the modern novel, from Fielding,
who began as Cervantes' professed imitator by lampooning Richardson, to
Jane Austen, who sharpened her acute discriminations on Gothic romances
and novels of sensibility:

> Charming as were all of Mrs. Radcliffe's works, and charming
> even as were the works of all her imitators, it was not in them
> perhaps that human nature, at least in the midland counties of
> England, was to be looked for.

The time, the place, and the style of *Northanger Abbey* have little in common
with Cervantes; but his protean formula has held, as it has been readjusted to
varying situations through the lengthy record of Don Quixote's posthumous
adventures. One of the many female Quixotes has been Madame Bovary; one
of the many Russian Quixotes has been Prince Myshkin. Heinrich Heine
summed up the romantic movement as a school of Quixotry when he
exclaimed: "Jean-Jacques Rousseau was my Amadís of Gaul!" In a parallel
vein, it might be argued that Voltaire's Amadís of Gaul was Leibniz, that
Tolstoy's was Napoleon, or Mark Twain's Baedeker. The number of specific
instances would seem to indicate some broader principle, such as André
Malraux has recently formulated in his illustrated treatise on the creative
imagination. His dictum—that every artist begins with *pastiche*—is highly
illuminating, so far as it goes; it has to be qualified only by recognizing that
pastiche implies both activities which we have associated and distinguished,
imitation and parody. The novelist must begin by playing the sedulous ape,
assimilating the craft of his predecessors; but he does not master his own
form until he has somehow exposed and surpassed them, passing from the
imitation of art through parody to the imitation of nature.

JOSÉ ORTEGA Y GASSET

The Hero

So far we have not had the opportunity of looking carefully at the essence of the comic. When I was writing that the novel shows us a mirage as such, the word *comedy* kept circling around the tip of my pen like a dog who hears his master's call. For some unknown reason a certain similarity makes us compare the mirage on the burnt-stubble fields with the comedies in the minds of men.

Now our story leads us back to this subject. We had left something hanging in mid-air, wavering between the room in the inn and Master Pedro's puppet show. This something is nothing less than the will of Don Quixote. People may be able to take good fortune away from this neighbor of ours, but they will not be able to take away his effort and courage. His adventures may be the vapors of a fermenting brain, but his will for adventure is real and true. Now, adventure is a dislocation of the material order, something unreal. In this will for adventure, in this effort and courage, we come across a strange dual nature, whose two elements belong to opposite worlds: the will is real but what is willed is not real.

Such a phenomenon is unknown in the epic. The men of Homer belong to the same world as their desires. In Don Quixote we have, on the other hand, a man who wishes to reform reality. But is he not a piece of that reality? Does he not live off it, is he not a consequence of it? How is it

From *Meditations on Quixote*. © 1961, 1989 by W. W. Norton and Co.

possible for that which does not exist—a projected adventure—to govern and alter harsh reality? Perhaps it is not possible, but it is a fact that there are men who decide not to be satisfied with reality. Such men aim at altering the course of things; they refuse to repeat the gestures that custom, tradition, or biological instincts force them to make. These men we call heroes, because to be a hero means to be one out of many, to be oneself. If we refuse to have our actions determined by heredity or environment it is because we seek to base the origin of our actions on ourselves and only on ourselves. The hero's will is not that of his ancestors nor of his society, but his own. This will to be oneself is heroism.

I do not think that there is any more profound originality than this "practical," active originality of the hero. His life is a perpetual resistance to what is habitual and customary. Each movement that he makes has first had to overcome custom and invent a new kind of gesture. Such a life is a perpetual suffering, a constant tearing oneself away from that part of oneself which is given over to habit and is a prisoner of matter.

HAROLD BLOOM

Cervantes: The Play of the World

We know more about Cervantes the man than we do about Shakespeare, and doubtless there is still much to be learned about him, because his life was vivid, arduous, and heroic. Shakespeare was an immense financial success as a playwright and died affluent, his societal ambitions (such as they were) fulfilled. Despite the popularity of *Don Quixote*, Cervantes received no royalties on it and had little luck with patrons. He had few realistic ambitions, beyond supporting himself and his family, and he failed as a playwright. Poetry was not his gift; *Don Quixote* was. Shakespeare's contemporary (they died, it is thought, on the same day), he has in common with Shakespeare the universality of his genius, and he is the only possible peer of Dante and Shakespeare in the Western Canon.

One thinks of him in conjunction with Shakespeare and Montaigne because the three of them are wisdom writers; there is no fourth so sane, temperate, and benign unless it be Molière, and in some sense he was Montaigne born again, but in another genre. In one respect, only Cervantes and Shakespeare occupy the highest eminence; you cannot get ahead of them, because they are always there before you.

Confronting the strength of *Don Quixote*, the reader is never lessened, only enhanced. This is not true in many moments of reading Dante or Milton or Jonathan Swift, whose *Tale of a Tub* always impresses me as the best

From *The Western Canon*. © 1994 by Harold Bloom.

prose in the language after Shakespeare's and yet reproves me incessantly. It is also not true of the experience of reading Kafka, the central writer of our chaos. Shakespeare is again the nearest analogue to Cervantes; we are sustained by the dramatist's well-nigh infinite capacity for disinterestedness. Although Cervantes is ceaselessly careful to be faithfully Catholic, we do not read *Don Quixote* as a pious work. Presumably Cervantes was an Old Christian, not descended from Jewish *conversos* or New Christians, yet we cannot be certain about his origins, just as we cannot hope to surmise his attitudes precisely. Characterizing his ironies is an impossible task; missing them is also impossible.

Despite his heroic war service (he permanently lost the use of his left hand at the great sea battle of Lepanto against the Turks), Cervantes had to be very wary of the Counter-Reformation and the Inquisition. Quixote's modes of madness grant him, and Cervantes, something of a fool's license, akin to that of the Fool in *King Lear*, a work staged simultaneously with the publication of the first part of *Don Quixote*. Cervantes was almost certainly a disciple of Erasmus, the Dutch humanist whose writing on Christian inwardness appealed greatly to the *conversos*, caught between a Judaism they had been forced to abandon and a Christian system that made them second-class citizens. Cervantes' ancestral family was crowded with physicians, a popular Jewish profession in Spain before the expulsions and forced conversions of 1492. A century later, Cervantes seems subtly haunted by that terrible year, which did much harm to Jews and Moors, as well as to Spain's well-being as an economy and a society.

No two readers ever seem to read the same *Don Quixote*, and the most distinguished critics have failed to agree on most of the book's fundamental aspects. Erich Auerbach thought it had no rival in the representation of ordinary reality as a continuous gaiety. Having just finished rereading *Don Quixote*, I blink at my inability to find what Auerbach called "so universal and multi-layered, so noncritical and nonproblematical a gaiety." "Symbolic and tragic terms," even when employed to categorize the hero's madness, seemed false to Auerbach. Against that claim I set the most poignant and Quixotic of all critical agonists, the Basque man of letters Miguel de Unamuno, whose "tragic sense of life" was founded upon his intimate relationship with Cervantes' masterpiece, which for Unamuno replaced the Bible as the authentic Spanish Scripture. "Our Lord Don Quixote," Unamuno called him, a Kafkan before Kafka, because his madness comes from a faith in what Kafka was to name "indestructibility." Unamuno's Knight of the Sorrowful Countenance is a quester for survival, whose only madness is a crusade against death: "Great was Don Quixote's madness, and it was great because the root from which it grew was great: the inextinguishable longing to survive, a source of the most extravagant follies as well as the most heroic acts."

In this view, the Don's madness is a refusal to accept what Freud called "reality testing," or the reality principle. When Don Quixote makes friends with the necessity of dying, he dies soon enough, thus returning to a Christianity conceived as the cult of death—and not just by Unamuno among Spanish visionaries. For Unamuno, the book's gaiety belongs solely to Sancho Panza, who purges his *daimon*, Don Quixote, and thus pleasurably follows the sad knight through every outrageous misadventure. This reading is again very close to Kafka's extraordinary parable, "The Truth about Sancho Panza," in which it is Sancho who has devoured all the romances of chivalry until his imagined demon, personified as the Don, departs upon his adventures with Sancho tagging along. Perhaps Kafka was making *Don Quixote* into one long and rather bitter Jewish joke, but that may be more faithful to the book than reading it with Auerbach as unalloyed gaiety.

Probably only *Hamlet* spurs as many variant interpretations as *Don Quixote* does. No one among us can purge Hamlet of his Romantic interpreters, and Don Quixote has inspired just as numerous and persistent a Romantic school of criticism, as well as books and essays opposing such a supposed idealization of Cervantes' protagonist. Romantics (myself included) see Quixote as hero, not fool; decline to read the book primarily as satire; and find in the work a metaphysical or visionary attitude regarding the Don's quest that makes the Cervantine influence upon *Moby-Dick* seem wholly natural. From the German philosopher critic Schelling in 1802 down to the Broadway musical *Man of La Mancha* in 1966, there has been a continuous exaltation of the supposedly impossible dream-quest. The novelists have been the major proponents of this apotheosis of Don Quixote: exuberant admirers have included Fielding, Smollett, and Sterne in England; Goethe and Thomas Mann in Germany; Stendhal and Flaubert in France; Melville and Mark Twain in the United States; and virtually all modern Hispanic American writers. Dostoevsky, who might seem the least Cervantine of writers, insisted that Prince Myshkin in *The Idiot* was modeled on Don Quixote. Since Cervantes' remarkable experiment is credited by many as having invented the novel, as opposed to the picaresque narrative, the devotion of so many later novelists is understandable enough; but the enormous passions evoked by the book, in Stendhal and Flaubert in particular, are extraordinary tributes to its achievement.

I myself naturally gravitate to Unamuno when I read *Don Quixote*, because for me the heart of the book is its revelation and celebration of heroic individuality, both in the Don and in Sancho. Unamuno rather perversely preferred the Don to Cervantes, but there I refuse to follow, because no writer has established a more intimate relation with his protagonist than Cervantes did. We wish we could know what Shakespeare himself thought of Hamlet; we know almost too much about how Don Quixote affected Cervantes, even if our knowledge is often indirect. Cervantes invented endless ways of disrupting his own narrative to compel the reader to tell the story in place of the wary author. The wily and wicked enchanters who supposedly work without ceasing to frustrate the magnificently indomitable Don Quixote are also employed to make us into unusually active readers. The Don supposes the sorcerers to exist, and Cervantes pragmatically realizes them as crucial components of his language. Everything is transformed through enchantment, is the Quixotic lament, and the wicked sorcerer is Cervantes himself. His characters have read all of the stories about one another, and much of the novel's second part concerns itself with their reactions to having read the first. The reader is educated into considerably more sophistication of response, even when Don Quixote stubbornly refuses to learn, though that refusal has more to do with his own "madness" than with the fictive status of the chivalric romances that have crazed him. The Don and Cervantes together evolve toward a new kind of literary dialectic, one that alternates in proclaiming both the potency and the vanity of the narrative in its relation to real events. Even as the Don, in part one, gradually comes to understand the limitations of fiction, so Cervantes grows in his pride of authorship and in the particular joy of having invented the Don and Sancho.

The loving, frequently irascible relationship between Quixote and Sancho is the greatness of the book, more even than the gusto of its representations of natural and social realities. What unites the Don and his squire is both their mutual participation in which has been called "the order of the play" and their equally mutual if rather grumpy affection for each other. I cannot think of a fully comparable friendship anywhere else in Western literature, certainly not one that relies so exquisitely upon hilarious conversation. Angus Fletcher, in his *Colors of the Mind*, catches the aura of these conversations:

> Where Quixote and Sancho meet is in a certain kind of animation, the spiritedness of their conversations. As they talk, and often debate vigorously, they enlarge the field of each other's thoughts. No thought on either side goes unchecked or uncritiqued. By mainly courteous disagreement, most courteous when most sharply in conflict, they gradually establish an area of free play, where thoughts are set free for us the readers to ponder.

My personal favorite among the many scores of Quixote-Sancho exchanges takes place in part two, chapter 28, after the knight has emulated Sir John Falstaff in the wisdom of discretion as the better part of valor. Unfortunately, his decision has involved abandoning a stunned Sancho to a furious village. After the incident, poor Sancho moans that he aches all over and receives rather pedantic comfort from the knight:

> "The reason for that," remarked Don Quixote, "is undoubtedly the fact that the club they used was a long one and caught you all the way down your back where those aching parts are located; and if it had gone any farther down, you would ache still more."
>
> "By God," exclaimed Sancho, "your Grace has taken a great load off my mind and made everything as clear as can be! Body of me! Is the cause of my pain such a mystery that it is necessary to explain to me that I ache wherever the club reached me?"

Hidden in this exchange is the bond between the two, who beneath the surface enjoy the intimacy of equality. We can defer the question of which is the more original figure, while noting that the allied figure that they constitute together is more original than either is alone. A loving but quarrelsome duo, Sancho and the Don are united by more than their mutual affection and their authentic respect for each other. At their best, they are companions in the order of play, a sphere with its own rules and its own vision of reality: Unamuno is again the useful Cervantine critic here, but the theoretician is Johan Huizinga in his subtle book, *Homo Ludens* (1944), which barely mentions Cervantes. Huizinga begins by asserting that his subject, play, is to be distinguished from both comedy and folly: "The category of the comic is connected with *folly* in the highest and lowest sense of that word. Play, however, is not foolish. It lies outside the antithesis of wisdom and folly."

Don Quixote is neither a madman nor a fool, but someone who plays at being a knight-errant. Play is a voluntary activity, unlike madness and foolishness. Play, according to Huizinga, has four principal characteristics: freedom, disinterestedness, excludedness or limitedness, and order. You can test all of these qualities upon the Don's knight-errantry, but not always upon Sancho's faithful service as squire, for Sancho is slower to yield himself to play. The Don lifts himself into ideal place and time and is faithful to his own freedom, to its disinterestedness and seclusion, and to its limits, until at last he is defeated, abandons the game, returns to Christian "sanity," and so dies. Unamuno says of Quixote that he went out to seek his true fatherland and found it in exile. As always, Unamuno understood what was most inward in the great book. The Don, like the Jews and the Moors, is an exile, but in the mode of the *conversos* and *moriscos*, an internal exile. Don Quixote leaves his village to seek his spirit's home in exile, because only exiled can he be free.

Cervantes never tells us explicitly why Alonso Quijano (the book gives the name several variant spellings) was first driven to craze himself by reading chivalric romances, until at last he went out upon the roads to become Don Quixote. A poor gentleman of La Mancha, Alonso has only one vice: he is an obsessive reader of the popular literature of the day, which crowds reality out of his mind. Cervantes describes Alonso as a pure case of the unlived life. He is single, close to fifty, presumably without sexual experience, confined to the company of a housekeeper in her forties, a nineteen-year-old niece, a field hand, and his two friends: the village curate and Nicholas the barber. Not far away lives a peasant girl, the robust Aldonza Lorenzo, who has unknowingly become the ideal object of his fantasies, renamed in them as the great lady, Dulcinea del Toboso.

Whether she is truly the object of the good man's quest is unclear. One critic has gone so far as to suggest that Quijano is impelled to become Don Quixote because of barely repressed lust for his own niece, a notion nowhere in Cervantes' text, but an indication of the desperation to which Cervantes has been known to drive his scholars. All Cervantes tells us is that his hero has gone mad, and we are given no clinical details whatsoever. Unamuno's reaction seems to me the best one on the Quixotic loss of his wits: "He lost them for our sake, for our benefit, so as to leave us an eternal example of spiritual generosity." That is to say, Don Quixote goes mad as a vicarious atonement for our drabness, our ungenerous dearth of imagination.

Sancho, a poor peasant, is persuaded to go along as squire on the knight's second sally, which turns into the glorious affair of the windmills. The inducement for the good and ostensibly slow-witted Sancho is that he will govern an island, which the knight will conquer for him. Cervantes is inevitably ironic when he first introduces us to Sancho, whose wit is extraordinary and whose true desire is to gain fame rather than wealth, as a governor. More fundamentally, an element in Sancho desires the order of play, uneasy as the rest of Sancho is with some of the consequences of Quixotic play. Like the Don, Sancho searches for a new ego, an idea that Alejo Carpentier, the Cuban novelist, believes Cervantes first invented. I would say that Shakespeare and Cervantes came at it simultaneously, the difference between the two being the modalities of change in their principal characters.

Don Quixote and Sancho Panza are each other's ideal conversationalist; they change by listening to each other. In Shakespeare change comes from self-overhearing and from pondering the implications of what one has heard. Neither the Don nor Sancho is capable of overhearing himself; the Quixotic ideal and the Panzaesque reality are too strong for their upholders to doubt, so they cannot absorb their own departures from their standards. They can speak blasphemies but not recognize them when they emerge. The tragic greatness of the Shakespearean protagonists extends to comedy, history, and romance; only in climactic recognition scenes are the survivors able to listen fully to what others are saying. Shakespeare's influence, and not just in English-speaking countries, has overcome that of Cervantes. Modern solipsism stems from Shakespeare (and from Petrarch before him). Dante, Cervantes, Molière—who depend on interchanges between their personae— seem less natural than Shakespeare's gorgeous solipsism, and perhaps they are indeed less natural.

Shakespeare has no parallel to the exchanges between the Don and Sancho, because his friends and lovers never quite listen to one another. Think of Anthony's death scene, in which Cleopatra hears and overhears mostly herself, or the attempts at play between Falstaff and Hal in which Falstaff is forced into defense because the prince so perpetually attacks. There are gentler exceptions, like Rosalind and Celia in *As You Like It*; but they are not the norm. Shakespearean individuality is matchless, but it exacts enormous costs. Cervantine egoism, exalted by Unamuno, is always qualified by the free relationship between Sancho and the Don, who grant one another space for play. Both Cervantes and Shakespeare are supreme in the creation of personality, but the greatest Shakespearean personalities— Hamlet, Lear, Iago, Shylock, Falstaff, Cleopatra, Prospero—at last wither gloriously in the air of an inward solitude. Don Quixote is saved by Sancho, and Sancho, by the Don. Their friendship is canonical and changes, in part, the subsequent nature of the canon.

What does madness mean if its sufferer cannot be deceived by other men or women? No one exploits Don Quixote, not even Quixote himself. He takes windmills for giants and puppet shows for realities, but he is not to be mocked, because he will outwit you. His madness is a *literary* madness and can be contrasted usefully to the only partly literary madness of the speaker in Robert Browning's great chivalric romance, "Childe Roland to the Dark Tower Came." Don Quixote is mad because his great prototype, the Orlando (Roland) of Ariosto's *Orlando Furioso*, fell into an erotic madness. So, as the Don points out to Sancho, did Amadis of Gaul, another heroic precursor. Browning's Childe Roland wants only to be "fit to fail," even as the poet-knights one by one failed before him at the Dark Tower. Don Quixote is considerably healthier than that; he wants to win, no matter how many times he gets painfully flattened. His madness, as he makes clear, is a poetic strategy worked out by others before him, and he is nothing if not a traditionalist.

Cervantes was wary of too close a Spanish precursor; his deepest affinities were with the *converso* Fernando de Rojas, author of the great narrative drama *Celestina*, not exactly a Catholic work in its savage amoralism and its lack of theological suppositions. Cervantes remarked that it "would be a divine book, in my view, if it concealed more the human," clearly meaning the refusal of human sexuality to accept any moral constraints. Don Quixote, of course, imposes moral constraints upon his sexual desires to such an extent that he might as well be a priest, which according to Unamuno he truly was: a priest of the true Spanish church, the Quixotic. The Don's perpetual eagerness for battle against nearly all odds is rather clearly a sublimation of the sexual drive. The obscure object of his desire, the enchanted Dulcinea, is the emblem of glory to be attained in and through violence, always rendered by Cervantes as an absurdity. A survivor of Lepanto and other battles, as well as of long years of Moorish captivity and then of Spanish prisons (where *Don Quixote* may have been begun), Cervantes had firsthand knowledge of battle and of bondage. We are intended to regard Don Quixote's shocking heroism with both great respect and considerable irony, a Cervantine stance not too easy to analyze. Outrageous as its manifestations are, the Don's courage convincingly surpasses that of any other hero in Western literature.

Direct confrontation of the greatness of *Don Quixote* cannot proceed very far without the critic's courage. Cervantes, with all his ironies, is in love with Don Quixote and Sancho Panza, and so is any reader who loves reading. Explaining love is a vain exercise in life, where the word "love" means everything and nothing but ought to be a rational possibility in regard to the greatest literature. Here Cervantes may have touched the universal more surely even than Shakespeare, since I remain bewildered that my intense love for Don Quixote's only rival among knights-errant, Sir John Falstaff, is not necessarily shared by all of my students, let alone by most of my fellow teachers. No one goes about calling Don Quixote "a disgusting and besotted old wretch," which was G. B. Shaw's judgment against Falstaff, but there are always Cervantine critics who persist in labeling the Don a fool and a madman, and who tell us that Cervantes is satirizing his hero's "undisciplined egocentricity." If that were true, there would be no book, for who wants to read about Alonso Quijano the Good? Disenchanted at the very end, he dies religiously and sanely, always reminding me of those friends of my youth who went through decades of psychoanalysis interminable, to terminate shrunken indeed and dried out, all passion spent, fit to die analytically and sanely. Even part one of the great book is anything but a satire on the hero, and part two, as is generally recognized, is so designed as to cause the reader an even firmer identification with the Don, and with Sancho.

Herman Melville, with authentic American gusto, called Don Quixote "that sagest sage that ever lived," happily ignoring the hero's fictiveness. There were for Melville three prime originals among literary characters: Hamlet, Don Quixote, and the Satan of *Paradise Lost*. Ahab, alas, was not quite a fourth—perhaps because he blended all three—but his crew acquired a Cervantine atmosphere, directly prayed for by Melville in a wonderful peroration that stations Cervantes, memorably and insanely, in the middle between the visionary of *Pilgrim's Progress* and President Andrew Jackson, hero of all American Democrats:

> Bear me out in it, thou great democratic God! who didst not refuse to the swart convict, Bunyan, the pale, poetic pearl; Thou who didst clothe with doubly hammered leaves of finest gold, the stumped and pauperized arm of old Cervantes; Thou who didst pick up Andrew Jackson from the pebbles; who didst hurl him upon a war-horse; who didst thunder him higher than a throne! Thou who, in all Thy mighty, earthly marchings, ever cullest Thy selectest champions from the kingly commons; bear me out in it, O God!

That is an ecstasy of the American religion, having little in common with the wary Catholicism of Cervantes, but much that is parallel with the Spanish religion of Quixotism as expounded by Unamuno. The tragic sense of life, discovered by Unamuno in *Don Quixote*, is also the faith of *Moby Dick*. Ahab is a monomaniac; so is the kindlier Quixote, but both are tormented idealists who seek justice in human terms, not as theocentric men but as ungodly, godlike men. Ahab seeks only Moby-Dick's destruction; renown is nothing to the Quaker captain, and revenge is everything.

No one, except a panoply of mythical enchanters, has done any harm to Don Quixote, who absorbs buffetings with endless stoicism. The Don's motive, according to Unamuno, is eternal fame, interpreted as "an expansion of the personality in space and time." I read that as the secular equivalent of the Blessing in the Yahwist: more life into a time without boundaries. Generosity and simple goodness are the Quixotic virtues. His vice, if there is one, is the Golden Age Spanish conviction that victory through arms is everything; but since he is so frequently defeated, this failing is transitory at worst.

As I do, Unamuno took most seriously the Don's sublimated desire for Aldonza Lorenzo and his subsequent Beatrice-like exaltation of her as the angelic if unfortunately enchanted Dulcinea, which allows us to see the knight in something close to his full complexity. He lives by faith while knowing, as his lucid outbursts show, that he believes in a fiction, and knowing—at least in flashes—that it is only a fiction. Dulcinea is a supreme fiction, and Don Quixote, an obsessed reader, is a poet of action who has created a grand myth. Unamuno's Quixote is a paradoxical agonist, the ancestor of the diminished questers who wander through our chaos in Kafka and Beckett. The hero of a secular "indestructibility" was perhaps unintended by Cervantes himself, but he achieves apotheosis in Unamuno's fiery commentary. This Quixote is a metaphysical actor, able to risk derision in order to keep idealism alive.

Against the idealistic knight of an essentially erotic faith, Cervantes sets the figure of the trickster, an extraordinary, quite Shakespearean character, Ginés de Pasamonte, who first appears in part one, chapter 22, as one of the prisoners bound for the galleys, and returns again in part two, chapters 25–27, as the illusionist Master Pedro, who divinates through a mystical monkey and then stages a puppet show so vivid that Don Quixote, mistaking it for his own reality, attacks and demolishes the puppets. In Ginés, Cervantes gives us an imaginary figure who would be as much at home in the Elizabethan underworld as in the lower depths of Golden Age Spain. When Don Quixote and Sancho first encounter him, he is being marched down a road together with a dozen other prisoners, all condemned by the king to service as galley slaves. The other culprits are handcuffed, and all are strung together by their necks on an iron chain. Ginés, the most formidable, is chained more extravagantly (unless otherwise indicated, I use here and throughout Samuel Putnam's translation):

> Back of these came a man around thirty years of age and of very good appearance, except that when he looked at you his eyes were seen to be a little crossed. He was shackled in a different manner from the others, for he dragged behind him a chain so huge that it was wrapped all around his body, with two rings at the throat, one of which was attached to the chain while the other was fastened to what is known as a keep-friend or friend's foot, from which two irons hung down to his waist, ending in handcuffs secured by a heavy padlock in such a manner that he could neither raise his hands to his mouth nor lower his head to reach his hands.

Ginés, as the guards explain, is famously dangerous, so bold and cunning that even chained as he is, they fear his escape. His sentence is ten years in the galleys, which is equivalent to civil death. The cruel inability of Ginés' head and hands to reach one another is, as Roberto González Echevarria notes, an irony directed against the authors of picaresque novels, for the picaroon Ginés is at work composing his own history, as he boasts:

> "If you want to know anything about my life, know that I am Ginés de Pasamonte whose life story has been written down by those fingers that you see here."
>
> "He speaks the truth," said the commissary, "for he has himself written his story, as big as you please, and has left the book in the prison, having pawned it for two hundred reales."
>
> "And I mean to redeem it," said Ginés, "even if it costs me two hundred ducats."
>
> "Is it as good as that?" inquired Don Quixote.
>
> "It is so good," replied Ginés, "that it will cast into the shade *Lazarillo de Tormes* and all others of that sort that have been or will be written. When I would tell you is that it deals with facts, and facts so interesting and amusing that no lies could equal them."
>
> "And what is the title of the book?" asked Don Quixote.
>
> "*The Life of Ginés de Pasamonte.*"
>
> "Is it finished?"
>
> "How could it be finished," said Ginés, "when my life is not finished as yet?"

The outrageous Ginés has stated a grand principle of the picaresque, one that does not apply to *Don Quixote*, even though that work too ends with the death of the hero. But Don Quixote dies metaphorically before Alonso Quijano the Good dies literally. *Lazarillo de Tormes*, the anonymous archetype of the Spanish picaresque, first published in 1553, remains wonderfully readable and was beautifully rendered into English by the poet W. S. Merwin in 1962. If the story of the boastful Ginés had been better than that, it would have been very good indeed; but of course it is, because it is part of *Don Quixote*. Ginés has done a previous four-year term in the galleys but is saved from his ten-year sentence through the intervention of the sublimely mad Quixote. Ginés and the other convicts escape, despite poor Sancho's desperate warning to his master that his action directly defies the king. Cervantes, himself a captive of the Moors for five years and imprisoned again in Spain for his supposed derelictions as a tax collector, clearly expresses a personal passion beyond irony in the speech of the Don that includes the plangent "There will be no dearth of others to serve his Majesty under more propitious circumstances; and it does not appear to me to be just to make slaves of those whom God created as free men."

After a general melee the guards run off, and the knight instructs the freed convicts to present themselves to Dulcinea, so as to describe the adventure. Ginés, after trying to talk sense to the soon infuriated Quixote, leads the convicts in stoning and stripping their savior and Sancho, before running off, until

> They were left alone now—the ass and Rocinante, Sancho and Don Quixote: the ass, crestfallen and pensive, wagging its ears now and then, being under the impression that the hurricane of stones that had raged about them was not yet over; Rocinante, stretched alongside his master, for the hack also had been felled by a stone; Sancho, naked and fearful of the Holy Brotherhood, and Don Quixote, making wry faces at seeing himself so mishandled by those to whom he had done so much good.

The pathos of this passage seems to me exquisite; it is one of those Cervantine effects that never leave one. Unamuno, as sublimely crazy as his lord, Don Quixote, delightfully comments, "All of which should teach us to liberate galley slaves precisely because they will not be grateful to us for it." The rueful Quixote disagrees with his Basque exegete and vows to Sancho that the lesson is learned, to which the wise squire ripostes, "If your Grace takes warning, then I am a Turk." It was Cervantes who took warning, because of his affection for his minor but superb creation, Ginés de Pasamonte, "the famous rogue and thief." Ginés, confidence man and shamanistic imp of the perverse, is what might be called one of the canonical criminal characters in literature, like Shakespeare's Barnardine in *Measure for Measure* or Balzac's superb Vautrin. If Vautrin can reappear as Abbé Carlos Herréra, then Ginés can manifest himself as Master Pedro, the puppet master. An important question to ask is what, besides the pride of authorship, impelled Cervantes to bring back Ginés de Pasamonte in part two of *Don Quixote*.

Critics generally agree that the contrast between Ginés and the Don, picaroon trickster and chivalric visionary, is partly an opposition of two literary genres, the picaresque and the novel, which Cervantes essentially invented, in much the same way that Shakespeare (who did not know Greek tragedy, only its crippled remnant in the Roman Seneca) invented modern tragedy and modern tragi-comedy as well. As in the Shakespearean protagonists, authentic inwardness incarnates itself in Don Quixote, whereas the scamp Pasamonte is all outwardness, despite his deep talents at duplicity. Ginés is a shapeshifter; he cannot change except in externals. The Don, like the great Shakespearean characters, cannot stop changing: that is the purpose of his frequently irascible but always finally loving conversations with the faithful Sancho. Bound together by the order of the play, they are also united by the endless further humanization they bring about in each other. Their crises are innumerable; how could they not be, in the realm of the Quixotic? Sancho hesitates sometimes on the verge of abandoning the relationship, yet he cannot; partly he is fascinated, but in the end he is held by love, and so is the Don. The love cannot perhaps be distinguished from the order of play, but that is as it should be. Certainly one reason for Ginés de Pasamonte's return in part two is that he never participates in play, even as puppet master.

Every reader recognizes that the difference between the two parts of *Don Quixote* is that everyone who matters most in part two is either explicitly credited with having read part one or knows that he was a character in it. That provides a different frame for the reappearance of the picaroon Ginés when we reach the moment in part two, chapter 25 when we encounter a man clad in chamois skin, hose, breeches, and a doublet, and with a patch of green taffeta over one eye and that whole side of his face. This is Master Pedro come, as he says, with the divining ape and the spectacle of the freeing of Melisendra by her husband, the famous knight-errant, Don Gaiferos, she being the daughter of Charlemagne held captive by the Moors, and he being a principal vassal of Charlemagne.

The landlord at the inn where Master Pedro joins Don Quixote and Sancho Panza says of the puppet master that "he talks more than six men, and drinks more than a dozen." After he identifies the Don and Sancho, at the advice of his divining ape (whose divination goes only backward, from present to past), Ginés-Pedro stages the puppet show, certainly one of the metaphorical splendors of Cervantes' masterpiece. The classic exegesis here is from Ortega y Gasset, in his *Meditations on Quixote*; he compares Master Pedro's puppet show to the Velázquez *Maids of Honor*, where the artist in painting the king and queen simultaneously places his studio in the picture. It is not a painting upon which Don Quixote could safely have gazed, and he is certainly the worst possible audience for the puppet show:

> Upon seeing such a lot of Moors and hearing such a din, Don Quixote thought that it would be a good thing for him to aid the fugitives; and, rising to his feet, he cried out, "Never so long as I live and in my presence will I permit such violence to be done to

so famous a knight and so bold a lover as Don Gaiferos. Halt, lowborn rabble; cease your pursuit and persecution, or otherwise ye shall do battle with me!"

With these words he drew his sword, and in one bound was beside the stage; and then with accelerated and unheard-of fury he began slashing at the Moorish puppets, knocking some of them over, beheading others, crippling this one, mangling that one. Among the many blows he dealt was one downward stroke that, if Master Pedro had not ducked and crouched, would have sliced off his head more easily that if it had been made of almond paste.

That downward stroke, by no means unintended, may be the heart of this delightful intervention. Master Pedro has intruded in the order of the play, where he has no place, and it moves to avenge itself upon the rogue. A while before, Don Quixote has said to Sancho that the puppet master must have made a bargain with the devil, because the divining ape "answers only questions about the past or the present, for that is as far as the devil's knowledge extends." The knight's suspicion of the trickster continues when he criticizes Master Pedro's mistakes in ascribing church bells to the Moorish mosques. Ginés-Pedro's defensive reply further prepares us for the Don's shattering of the show:

> "Don't be looking for trifles, Señor Don Quixote, or expect things to be impossibly perfect. Are not a thousand comedies performed almost every day that are full of inaccuracies and absurdities, yet they run their course and are received not only with applause but with admiration and all the rest? Go on, boy, and let him talk; for so long as I fill my wallet, it makes no difference if there are as many inaccuracies in my show as there are motes in the sun."

Don Quixote's reply is the grimly laconic: "You have spoken the truth." Here Master Pedro has become Cervantes' great literary rival, the monstrously productive and successful poet-playwright Lope de Vega, whose financial triumphs heightened Cervantes' sense of commercial failure as a stage dramatist. The knight's subsequent assault upon pasteboard illusions is at once a critique of public taste and a metaphysical manifestation of Quixotic or visionary will, making ghostlier the demarcations between art and nature. The humor of disjunction is salted by literary satire, hardly mitigated by the aftermath in which the chastened Don makes financial amends for his generous error and blames the usual wicked enchanters for having deceived him. Ginés de Pasamonte then vanishes from the story, for he has performed his function as picaroon foil to the visionary knight. We are left with not only delight, but an aesthetic fable that goes on reverberating as an epitome of the Quixotic enterprise, showing at once its limits and its heroic persistence at breaking beyond the normative boundaries of literary representation. Ginés, archetype of the picaresque, cannot compete with the Don, forerunner of the triumph of the novel.

Readers divide over their preference for part one or part two of *Don Quixote*, perhaps because these are not only very different works but curiously separate from each other, not so much in tone and attitude as in the relation of the Don and Sancho to their world. I do not hear any weariness in Cervantes in part two (which I prefer), but knight and squire alike have to sustain a new self-consciousness, and sometimes they seem to take this as an implicit burden. To know that you are a character in an ongoing book is not always a help in your adventures. Surrounded by readers of their earlier debacles, Don Quixote and Sancho nevertheless remain uninhibited. Sancho actually gains in zest, and there is an even greater closeness in friendship between the two characters. Best of all, there is Sancho on his own, during his ten days of being a wise and much-harried governor, until he sensibly resigns and returns to Don Quixote and to himself. What happens to Cervantes in this part moves me most, because his relation to his own writing changes. He is facing toward death, and something of him (as he knows) will die with Don Quixote, while something else, perhaps deeper, will live on in Sancho Panza.

Cervantes' relation to his enormous book is never easy to categorize. Leo Spitzer saw it as conferring a new if carefully limited authority on the literary artist:

> High above this worldwide cosmos of his making . . . Cervantes's artistic self is enthroned, an all-embracing creative self, Nature-like, God-like, almighty, all wise, all good—and benign . . . this artist is God-like but not deified. . . . Cervantes always bows before the supernal wisdom of God, as embodied in the teachings of the Catholic Church and the established order of the state and of society.

Whether or not he was descended from Jewish forced converts, Cervantes would have been suicidal not to so bow, as Spitzer surely knew. Whatever *Don Quixote* is or is not, it is scarcely a Catholic devotional novel, or a paean to "sovereign reason," as Spitzer also suggested. The book's continuous laughter is frequently melancholy, even painful, and Don Quixote is both a stalwart of humane affection and a man of sorrow. Can the "peculiarly Cervantean" ever be defined? Erich Auerbach said that it "cannot be described in words" but courageously tried anyway:

> It is not a philosophy; it is no didactic purpose; it is not even a being stirred by the uncertainty of human existence or by the power of destiny, as in the case of Montaigne and Shakespeare. It is an attitude—an attitude toward the world, and hence also toward the subject matter of his art—in which bravery and equanimity play a major part. Together with the delight he takes in the multifariousness of his sensory play there is in him a certain Southern reticence and pride. This prevents him from taking the play very seriously.

I confess that these eloquent sentences do not describe the *Don Quixote* I persist in rereading, if only because Cervantes seems to take the play of the world and the counterplay of Don Quixote and Sancho Panza very seriously as well as ironically. The Cervantean is as multivalent as the Shakespearean: it contains us, with all of our severe differences from one another. Wisdom is as much an attribute of the Don and Sancho, particularly when they are considered together, as intelligence and mastery of language are qualities of Sir John Falstaff, Hamlet, and Rosalind. Cervantes' two heroes are simply the largest literary characters in the whole Western Canon, except for their triple handful (at most) of Shakespearean peers. Their fusion of folly and wisdom and their disinterestedness can be matched only in Shakespeare's most memorable men and women. Cervantes has naturalized us as Shakespeare has: we can no longer see what makes *Don Quixote* so permanently original, so searchingly strange a work. If the play of the world can still be located in the greatest literature, then it must be here.

Chronology

1547   Miguel de Cervantes Saavedra born in Alcalá de Henares to Rodrigo de Cervantes and Leonora de Cortinas, fourth in a family of seven. Baptized October 6.

1568   Cervantes's poems are included in a volume published to commemorate the death of Queen Isabel de Valois, third wife of Philip II.

1569   Travels to Rome, Italy, possibly becoming a soldier in the service of Cardinal Giulio Acquaviva.

1571   Performs heroic service on the ship *Marquesa* at the battle of Lepanto, October 7. Wounded during the battle, he loses the use of his left hand.

1575   While returning to Spain with his brother Rodrigo, their ship *El Sol* is captured by Barbary pirates. The two brothers are taken to Algiers as slaves.

1575–80 Captive in Algiers where he unsuccessfully organizes four attempts to escape with his fellow Christian prisoners. (This experience later becomes the model for *Don Quixote* I, 39–41.)

1577   Rodrigo released, leaves for Spain to arrange rescue of his brother, which fails.

1580   Miguel de Cervantes ransomed by a Trinitarian Friar, Juan Gil.

1581–87   After secret service in Portugal and Oran, Miguel de Cervantes attempts a literary career in Madrid as a dramatist with little success; begins affair with Ana Franca de Rojas, who would eventually give birth to his illegitimate daughter, Isabel de Saavedra.

1584   Publishes pastoral novel *La Galatea*; marries Catalina de Salazar y Palacios, eighteen years his junior.

1587–95   Becomes a purchasing agent for the Spanish Armada and later becomes an itinerant collector of supplies, mostly in Andalusia. Implicated in legal and financial difficulties concerning the keeping of accounts; begins career as a stage dramatist, writing between twenty and thirty plays between 1585 and 1600. Few are successful.

1597   Arrested in Seville for alleged malfeasance; released on the first of December.

1605   Arrested for a second time, this time in connection with the death of a young nobleman, and transferred to a prison at Valladolid, the capital of Spain; begins writing *Don Quixote* in prison; Part one of *Don Quixote* is published (the publisher holds all rights to the work). A second edition is issued in Madrid later in the year.

1606   Cervantes and his family move to Madrid; begins work on *Novelas ejemplares* (*Exemplary Novels*), a collection of 12 short stories.

1613   *Exemplary Novels* published; Cervantes becomes a member of the Franciscan Tertiaries at Alcalá de Henares and a pensioner of the Count of Lemos.

1614   Allegorical poem *Viaje del Parnaso* (*Journey to Parnassus)* is published; the "false Quixote" published at Tarragona by the otherwise unknown and perhaps pseudonymous Alonso Fernández de Avellaneda. This plagarism inspires Cervantes to complete his own work.

1615   Cervantes's part two of *Don Quixote* is published; *Ocho comedias, y ocho entremeses nuevos* (*Eight Comedies and Eight Interludes, Never Before Performed*) is published.

1616   Cervantes dies on April 22. (Tradition has it that he died on the 23rd, but that is the day his burial certificate indicates that he was buried.)

1617   *Los trabajos de Persiles y Sigismunda* (*The Travails of Persiles and Sigismunda*), a verse romance, is published posthumously.

Contributors

HAROLD BLOOM is Sterling Professor of the Humanities at Yale University and Henry W. and Albert A. Berg Professor of English at the New York University Graduate School. He is the author of over 20 books, including *Shelley's Mythmaking* (1959), *The Visionary Company* (1961), *Blake's Apocalypse* (1963), *Yeats* (1970), *A Map of Misreading* (1975), *Kabbalah and Criticism* (1975), *Agon: Toward a Theory of Revisionism* (1982), *The American Religion* (1992), *The Western Canon* (1994), and *Omens of Millennium: The Gnosis of Angels, Dreams, and Resurrection* (1996). *The Anxiety of Influence* (1973) sets forth Professor Bloom's provocative theory of the literary relationships between the great writers and their predecessors. His most recent books include *Shakespeare: The Invention of the Human*, a 1998 National Book Award finalist, and *How to Read and Why*, which was published in 2000. In 1999, Professor Bloom received the prestigious American Academy of Arts and Letters Gold Medal for Criticism.

MIGUEL DE UNAMUNO (1864–1936) was an influential Spanish poet, playwright, essayist, and moralist. His philosophy found the fullest expression in *The Tragic Sense of Life in Men and Peoples* (1913). His most famous novel is *Abel Sánchez* (1917), a modern retelling of the biblical story of Cain and Abel.

THOMAS MANN (1875–1955) is considered the greatest German novelist of the 20th century. His early novels—*Buddenbrooks* (1900), *Death in Venice* (1912), and *The Magic Mountain* (1924)—earned him the Nobel Prize for Literature in 1929. His later novels include *Joseph and His Brothers* (1933), *Lotte in Weimar* (1939), *Doktor Faustus* (1947), and *The Confessions of Felix*

Krull, Confidence Man (1954). His many essays on literature appear in *Essays of Three Decades*.

FRANZ KAFKA (1883–1924) was a Czech-born German writer of visionary fictions, whose posthumously published novels—*The Trial* (1925), *The Castle* (1926), and *America* (1927)—express the anxieties of 20th-century man.

ERICH AUERBACH (1892–1957) taught in Germany, Turkey, and the United States. He published his major work *Mimesis: The Representation of Reality in Western Literature* in 1946 (English translation, 1953). His other important works concern Dante, Vico, and Romance philology.

WYSTEN HUGH (W. H.) AUDEN (1907–1973) was a distinguished Anglo-American poet and man of letters who wrote many essays on literary subjects. His critical essays can be found in *The Dyer's Hand* (1962).

VLADIMIR NABOKOV (1899–1977) was a Russian-born novelist and critic, who wrote both in Russian and English. His best works, including *Lolita* (1955), are written with idiosyncratic literary effects. His major works include the novels *The Gift* (1937), *The Real Life of Sebastian Knight* (1941), *Pnin* (1957), and *Pale Fire* (1962). *Lectures on Literature* (1980) was published after his death.

JORGE LUIS BORGES (1899–1986) was an Argentine poet, essayist and short-story writer. His best fantastic stories are collected in the series of *Ficcione* ("Fictions"; 1944) and the volume of English translation entitled *The Aleph and Other Stories, 1933–1969*, published in 1970. A 1952 collection of essays, *Other Inquisitions, 1937–1952*, reveals him at his analytical best.

MARK VAN DOREN (1894–1972) was an American poet and critic. His books include *Enjoying Poetry, American and British Literature since 1890* (1925), *Walt Whitman, Man, Poet, Philosopher* (1977), and the poetry collections *Harmony of Morning, 7 PM and Other Poems* (1926), and *Good Morning: Last Poems* (1973).

HARRY LEVIN was Irving Babbitt Professor of Comparative Literature at Harvard University. His works include *James Joyce: A Critical Introduction* (1941), *Contexts of Criticism* (1957), and *The Gates of Horn: A Study of Five French Realists* (1963), as well as studies of Christopher Marlowe and *Hamlet*.

JOSÉ ORTEGA Y GASSET (1883–1955) was a Spanish philosopher and humanist who greatly influenced the cultural renaissance of Spain in the 20th century. His best known works are *Meditations on Don Quixote* (1914), *Modern Theme* (1923), and *The Revolt of the Masses* (1929).

Bibliography

Allen, John J. *Don Quixote: Hero or Fool? A Study in Narrative Technique*. Gainesville: University Presses of Florida, 1969.

Bell, Aubrey. *Cervantes*. Norman: University of Oklahoma Press, 1947.

Bjornson, Richard, ed. *Approaches to Teaching Cervantes's Don Quixote*. New York: Modern Language Association of America, 1984.

Byron, William. *Cervantes, A Biography*. Garden City, N.Y.: Doubleday, 1978.

Cascardi, Anthony J. *The Bounds of Reason: Cervantes, Dostoevsky, Flaubert*. New York: Columbia University Press, 1986.

Church, Margaret. *Don Quixote: The Knight of La Mancha*. New York: New York University Press, 1971.

Close, Anthony J. "Don Quixote as a Burlesque Hero: A Reconstructed Eighteenth Century View." *Forum for Modern Languages* 10 (1974): 365–78.

———. *The Romantic Approach to* Don Quixote: *A Critical History of the Romantic Tradition in Quixote Criticism*. Cambridge: Cambridge University Press, 1978.

———. "Sancho Panza: Wise Fool." *Modern Language Review* 68 (1973): 344–57.

Cox, Ralph Merrit. *The Rev. John Bowle: The Genesis of Cervantean Criticism*. Chapel Hill: University of North Carolina Press, 1971.

Drake, Dana B. *Don Quijote in World Literature: A Selective Annotated Bibliography*. New York: Garland, 1980.

Durán, Manuel. *Cervantes*. New York: Twayne, 1974.

Efron, Arthur. *Don Quixote and the Dulcineated World*. Austin: University of Texas Press, 1971.

El Saffar, Ruth S. *Beyond Fiction: The Recovery of the Feminine in the Novels of Cervantes*. Berkeley: University of California Press, 1984.

———. "Distance and Control in *Don Quixote*: A Study in Narrative Technique." *North Carolina Studies in the Romance Languages and Literature*, no. 147. Chapel Hill: University of North Carolina Department of Romance Languages, 1975.

———. "The Function of the Fictional Narrator in *Don Quixote*" *MLN* 83 (1968): 165–77.

Entwistle, William J. *Cervantes*. Oxford: Clarendon, 1940.

Flores, Angel, and M. J. Bernadete, eds. *Cervantes Across the Centuries: A Quadricentinnial Volume*. New York, Dryden Press, 1947.

Fuentes, Carlos. *Don Quixote: Or, the Critique of Reading*. Austin: Institute of Latin American Studies, University of Texas at Austin, 1976.

Grismer, Raymond L. *Cervantes: A Bibliography*. New York: Kraus, 1946.

Johnson, Caesar. *Madness and Lust: A Psychoanalytic Approach to* Don Quixote. Berkeley: University of California Press, 1983.

Karl, Frederick R. "Don Quixote as Archetypal Artist and *Don Quixote* as Archetypal Novel." In *The Adversary Literature*. New York: Farrar, Straus & Giroux, 1974.

Ledesma, Francisco Navarro. *Cervantes: The Man and the Genius*. Translated and revised by Don Gabriela Bliss. New York: Charter House, 1973.

Lewis, Dominic Bevan Wyndham. *The Shadow of Cervantes*. London: Hollis and Carter, 1962.

Linsalata, Carmine Rocca. *Smolett's Hoax: Don Quixote in English*. Palo Alto: Stanford University Press, 1956.

Madariaga, Salvador de. *Don Quixote: An Introductory Essay in Psychology*. London: Oxford University Press, 1961.

Mades, Leonard. *The Armor and the Brocade: A Study of Don Quixote and the Courtier*. New York: Las Americas, 1968.

Mancing, Howard. *The Chivalric World of Don Quixote: Style, Structure and Narrative Technique*. Columbia: University of Missouri Press, 1982.

McKendrick, Melveena. *Cervantes*. Boston: Little, Brown, 1980.

Murillo, Louis Andrew. *The Golden Dial: Temporal Configuration in* Don Quixote. Oxford: Dolphin Books, 1975.

Plaja, Arturo Serrano. *"Magic" Realism in Cervantes: Don Quixote As Seen through Tom Sawyer and The Idiot*. Translated by Robert S. Rudder. Berkeley: University of California Press, 1970.

Predmore, Richard Lionel. *Cervantes*. New York: Dodd, Mead, 1973.

———. *The World of Don Quixote*. Cambridge: Harvard University Press, 1967.

Riley, Edward. *Cervantes's Theory of the Novel*. Oxford: Clarendon, 1962.

Robert, Marthe. *The Old and the New: From Don Quixote to Kafka*. Berkeley: University of California Press, 1977.

Siciliano, Ernest A. *The Jesuits in the Quijote and Other Essays*. Barcelona, Spain: Ediciones Hispam, 1974.

Ullman, Pierre L. "Romanticism and Irony in *Don Quixote*: A Continuing Controversy." *Papers on Language and Literature* 17 (Summer 1981): 320–33.

Wardropper, Bruce W. "*Don Quixote*: Story or History?" *Modern Philology* 63 (August 1965): 1–11.

Weiger, John G. "*Don Quixote*: The Comedy in Spite of Itself." *Bulletin of Hispanic Studies* 60 (October 1983): 283–92.

———. *The Substance of Cervantes*. New York: Cambridge University Press, 1985.

Welsh, A. *Reflections on the Hero as Quixote*. Princeton: Princeton University Press, 1981.

Willis, Raymond Smith. *The Phantom Chapters of the Quijote*. New York: Hispanic Institute, 1953.

Acknowledgments

"Glosses on *Don Quixote*" by Miguel de Unamuno. From *Our Lord Don Quixote: The Life of Don Quixote and Sancho with Related Essays*. © 1967 by the Bollingen Foundation. Reprinted with permission.

"Voyage with Don Quixote" by Thomas Mann. From *Essays of Three Decades*. © 1929, 1933, 1934, 1947 Alfred A. Knopf. Reprinted with permission.

"The Truth about Sancho Panza" by Franz Kafka. From *Parables*. (Translated by Willa and Edwin Muir.) © 1946, 1947 Schocken Books Inc. Reprinted with permission.

"The Enchanted Dulcinea" by Erich Auerbach. From *Mimesis: The Representation of Reality in Western Literature*. © 1953 by Princeton University Press. Reprinted with permission.

"The Ironic Hero: Some Reflections on Don Quixote" by W. H. Auden. From *Horizon* 20. © 1949 by *Horizon*. Reprinted with permission.

"Cruelty and Mystification" by Vladimir Nabokov. From *Lectures on Don Quixote*. © 1983 by the Estate of Vladimir Nabokov. Reprinted with permission.

"Pierre Menard, Author of Don Quixote" by Jorge Luis Borges. From *Ficciones*. © 1962 by Grove Press Inc. Reprinted with permission.

"Don Quixote's Profession" by Mark Van Doren. From *Don Quixote's Profession*. © 1958 Columbia University Press. Reprinted with permission.

"The Example of Cervantes" by Harry Levin. From *Contexts of Criticism* (Cambridge, Mass.: Harvard University Press, 1957). © 1957 by the President and Fellows of Harvard College. Reprinted with permission.

"The Hero" by José Ortega y Gasset. From *Meditations on Quixote*. © 1961 and renewed 1989 by W. W. Norton & Co. Reprinted with permission.

"Cervantes: The Play of the World" by Harold Bloom. From *The Western Canon*. © 1994 by Harold Bloom. Reprinted with permission.

Index